DATING DADDY

DATING DADDY

REALIZING GOD AS FATHER THROUGH DADDY ISSUES AND BAD ROMANCE

Shavonne L. Holton, M.S. Ed.

Foreword by Kenneth E. Sullivan Jr.

VK Press, LLC
PO BOX 78044
Indianapolis, IN 46278
www.vkpresses.com

Dating Daddy: Realizing God as Father through Daddy Issues and Bad Romance is a work of nonfiction. Some names and identifying details have been changed.

Copyright © 2017 by Shavonne Holton

All rights reserved. No part of this book may be reproduced or transmitted in any form or by any means, graphic, electronic, or mechanical including photocopying, recording, taping or by any information storage and retrieval system, without the written permission of the publisher, except where permitted by law.

If you would like to do any of the above, please seek permission first by contacting VK Press, LLC.

Scripture taken from the New King James Version®. Copyright © 1982 by Thomas Nelson. Used by permission. All rights reserved.

Excerpts from American Psychological Association were reprinted with permission. APA is not responsible for the accuracy of this translation.

Excerpts from "The Myth of the Missing Black Father" by Roberta Coles and Charles Green (editors). Copyright © 2010 Columbia University Press. Reprinted with permission of the publisher.

Editor: Sophia Muthuraj
Copyeditor: Janet Schwind
Cover Photo: Lacoiya Reed
Cover Design: Sylvia "Ess" Rivers
Interior Design: Suzanne Parada

First edition published February 10, 2017 in the United States by VK Press, LLC

E-Book ISBN 978-0-9982754-0-6
Paperback ISBN 978-0-9982754-1-3
Hardcover ISBN 978-0-9982754-2-0

To my GPa, Charles Jackson, you are my favorite movie date. I love you and am thankful for your love during the peaks and valleys of life.

*To my niece, Shayla Marie Newman, your smile lights my life. May your worst struggle be in choosing the best of the best possibilities.
I love you.*

CONTENTS

FOREWORD I
PREFACE III
INTRODUCTION IX

JEHOVAH-JIREH, MY PROVIDER
Chapter 1 | Our Father, Which Art in Heaven 2
Chapter 2 | Father(s) for the Fatherless 11
Chapter 3 | Making Meaning of God, the Provider 21

DAD: MODEL OF MANHOOD
Chapter 4 | Honoring an Absent Father 30
Chapter 5 | Silver Lining 41
Chapter 6 | Insight from Dad's Knee 52

CLIFF: DATING FOR DADDY HEARTBREAK
Chapter 7 | Love Escapade 62
Chapter 8 | Can You See (The Real) Me? 73
Chapter 9 | Lessons in Love 84

LEO: DATING DADDY'S SUBSTITUTE
Chapter 10 | Age Ain't Nothing but a Number 94
Chapter 11 | Nature of the Chase 105
Chapter 12 | Word to the Wise 115

DEION: DATING FOR DADDY POTENTIAL
Chapter 13 | Love and Football 124
Chapter 14 | Gone AWOL 135
Chapter 15 | Loving on Eggshells 146
Chapter 16 | Unraveling a Fortuitous Marriage 156

GOD, AS FATHER

Chapter 17 | A Close Father 166
Chapter 18 | A Father's Joy: Daughter's Restoration 176
Chapter 19 | Shadow of Death 186
Chapter 20 | Learning to Let Go 198

RENEWED DAUGHTER

Chapter 21 | Built to Last 210

ADDENDUM: Being a Loving Bystander 222
ACKNOWLEDGEMENTS 224
NOTES 227
ABOUT THE AUTHOR 233

Tough times don't last, but tough people do!
~Sister Pamela Maddox, Minister

FOREWORD

I can truly say as a proud father of two beautiful daughters that daughters are truly a gift from God. Every daughter possesses a unique personality and set of gifts. They not only need the loving example of a mother, but they need the assurance of a father. Every single woman needs a platonic relationship with a man—particularly with her father. A father should be the first person to take his daughter on a date. He sets the standard for the type of man a woman will look for and, in many cases, choose to date and marry. The father-daughter relationship allows a daughter to gain important insight and information that will help her build the healthy solid relationships God intended for her to have.

It's sad to say that too many young ladies in our day and age suffer from what I refer to as a daddy deficit, and they grow up without a healthy relationship with their father. Too often this causes many young ladies to search for affection, assurance and affirmation from all the wrong men, leading many young ladies down a road of abuse, pain and hurt.

Dating Daddy does a great job of giving therapeutic words of encouragement. Shavonne is very candid in terms of sharing her personal ups and downs and pains and struggles, victories and life experiences. She provides young women with invaluable insight and information as she shares her own real-life relationship experiences. We see a young woman who has stumbled along the way as she searched for real love and she emerges triumphantly with greater confidence, self-esteem and self-awareness!

I highly recommend this book and believe it is a definite must-read for every young lady whether or not they have had a healthy relationship with their father. This book helps young ladies discover their worth and value and helps them to discover how to navigate some of the relationship challenges they may face. I believe this book is also important and helpful for young men and fathers to read to better understand our responsibility to our daughters, wives, significant others and all the ladies in our lives whom we love. In 1 Peter 3:7, the Bible admonishes men to dwell with their wives with understanding. This book helps to provide men with a more in-depth understanding of the complexities and unique needs of the women in our lives. I enjoyed every moment of reading and believe you will as well. Get ready for a read that will stimulate your thinking, arouse your emotions and challenge your actions.

Pastor Kenneth E. Sullivan, Jr.
Senior Pastor of New Direction Church

PREFACE

You probably picked up this book because the title gripped you or the topic is something you've wanted to make sense of for quite some time. As you may know, we cannot underestimate the significance of the father-daughter connection in establishing the standards for future romantic relationships. Journalist and founder of the Daddy's Promise initiative, Ed Gordon, states, "Many times the expectation of how a man treats a woman and how a woman treats a man is derived from the interaction or lack thereof a woman had with her father." This quote really resonates with me since I grew up without a father and had to learn the lessons a father teaches his daughter through role models, men in the church, family members, and by trial and error in my own relationships.

For instance, my first long-term relationship was with my college sweetheart, Cliff. Our bond was an emotionally turbulent one because I was challenged to let go of all the hurt and false sense of self-reliance that kept me guarded and made my heart impenetrable. The turbulence was caused by his unending love for me and his unwillingness to let me go no matter how much I pushed him away, figuratively and literally. At the time Cliff and I were seeing each other, it was not clear if there was a connection between the model set by my father and the qualities of Cliff I so adored.

Around 2006 I began to question my personal criteria for the men I chose to date, and at that time I was dating a man named Leo, who was old enough to be my father. Even though I'm writing the book now, ten years later, the seed for it was planted when I was with Leo. It was then that I wondered if I was looking for qualities my own biological father possessed. Was my father's lack of involvement creating a set of unspoken criteria of its own? I don't know, but it was not until later I'd realize Leo possessed certain qualities I wished were present in my father.

Almost ten years from the moment I met Leo, as my marriage to Deion was dissolving, I thought about my relationship with my father again. My upbringing was such a rocky road that I sought stability in my relationship with Deion. One of his most attractive qualities was that he possessed the love, leadership, and warmth I would have desired for the father of my future children. But when our marriage failed I wondered, *Is he just like my father but with a different name?* The ending of our union prompted me to investigate the implications of the father-daughter relationship on my romantic relationships.

It was during this quest that I had a life-changing spiritual epiphany. For years, I recall other Christians' default response to hard times was to pray to our Heavenly "Father," but I never understood what this meant. My view of God was limited and circumstantial. What did it mean to see Him as a father? What does it mean to have the unconditional love of a supreme being when you do not have a tangible example of a father figure? What I realized was that not only had my father's absence impacted my choices in relationships, but it also affected me spiritually. I was unable to see God as a father because I did not understand a father's unconditional love for his daughter.

Therefore, this book is a journey from my earlier understandings of God through the epiphany that led to my understanding of him as my Father and the subsequent beginning of my healing process following my divorce. I also include a description of my relationship with my own father to make sense of the romantic connections that have impacted me most. While I highlight some of the role models and family members who had filled in the gap as surrogate father figures in my life, I would be remiss if I did not acknowledge the women who have shaped and supported my development into the woman I am today.

Had I written this book when I initially thought of the concept, it would have been incomplete. First, my writing has improved SIGNIFICANTLY from the time I initially thought about writing it ten years ago. Also, I had more living to do. I needed to experience more of life to add depth and breadth to my testimony. Furthermore, my graduate school program in higher education trained me to reflect on my practical experiences with the support of research.

As such, this book is not merely an anecdotal account but is supported through psychological and sociological scholarship. Nor is it a tell-all that seeks to paint the characters of my life in the most negative light possible while hiding my own flaws—but is actually undergirded by some of the most compelling lessons I've learned from sermons and spiritual literature that have guided my life experiences. I love quotes and was intentional in selecting the wisdom, sayings, and epigraphs shared in this work.

I identify myself as Black, woman, Christian, artist, scholar, chameleon, weightlifter, and daughter of an absent father, to name a few. As a unique individual, I faced distinctive challenges resulting from all the ways I identify myself and who I became as a consequence of my upbringing. This book explores various facets of my identity and how these characteristics were in concert or out of sync at any given season of my life. Though you may find connections to your experiences in love and relating to others, I challenge you to reflect on your own journey in your own way in your own time.

This is not your typical Christian book as it details a raw perspective that is not typically shared from a more conservative pulpit on Sunday morning. I believe that I am a woman of good character, but there are stories I will share that do not paint me as the most virtuous woman. Some details have been excluded to protect the identity of the people who are mentioned, but I was as transparent as I could be to show God's unlimited grace. If a doctor is unable to treat a patient based off knowing only half of their symptoms, how can I expect God to use my story for good if I only shared the favorable parts? There is power in testimonials! Ultimately, this book is a reflection of my experience. My hope is that all daughters who grew up without a close relationship with their fathers can reflect on their own choices in love and the importance of establishing one's own identity in God before pursuing a meaningful relationship with another human being: friend, foe, or in love.

The memoir is divided into six sections. The first section is a glance into the origins of my relationship with God, and by the sixth section you see how it comes full circle—my relationship with Him deepened into a father-daughter relationship. The second section covers my earthly father and our relationship, which will serve as a lens for my relationships with Cliff, Leo, and Deion in sections three, four, and five, respectively.

Each section is broken down into three or more chapters. There is a chapter in each section that gives a brief background on the relationship. Another chapter highlights the theme of that relationship as supported by research or biblical stories. Finally, in the last chapter I share insights or lessons learned from each of the relationships.

In the sixth section that details my understanding of God as Father, I weaved in another story that was critical to include. It was the time where I went from broken to beyond broken and numb within a short timeframe and had a life-altering epiphany that changed the trajectory of my life. A common misconception about Christianity is that one will never experience tough times if they "just had Jesus." But nothing could be further from the truth. As you will see, even after I recommitted myself to seeking God daily, I faced some of the darkest days of my life.

Writing this memoir has proven to be a healing process for me and I want to acknowledge the early contributors to this work. I am especially grateful to my absolute best sistah-friends Tamara Jordan and Manon Bullock for their unending love and support throughout my healing process. You both sacrificed so much to bring me back to life. I thank God for blessing me with women who remind me of His love and grace. You have ridden this rollercoaster of life with me and have earned your keep! I absolutely love you two! To my pastor, Kenneth E. Sullivan Jr., I thank God for ministering through you as I transitioned to this new phase of my journey.

Before you read any further, remember what Jesus told the scribes and the Pharisees: "He who is without sin, cast the first stone" (John 8: 7). This preface is your basket to drop any stones and judgments before proceeding into this journey. Without further ado, this is my story...

INTRODUCTION

"How do I do this when my marriage is falling apart?" I desperately asked Chrisette over the phone in tears. We had been friends since freshman year of high school. She was my maid of honor when I married Deion a little over a year and a half ago. We were so close that I told Deion if he ever planned to propose to me, it was mandatory that she was there.

In the calmest voice, Chrisette responded, "You should do it for you. This will be good for you."

How could any of this be good for me? I thought.

The timing of this wedding-inspired photoshoot was more than ironic. In fact, it seemed outright cruel of life that this shoot would take place while my own marriage was on the rocks!

* * *

Just a few months earlier, at the onset of summer 2015, my friend Toy had asked if I could model my wedding gown for a marketing campaign to advertise her budding event planning business. She said she would provide makeup artists, hair stylists and accessories, and my only responsibility would be to bring my wedding gown. Without hesitation, I had accepted. I was excited to showcase my long, full, flawlessly white Alfred Angelo dress with a sweetheart neckline that accentuated the fullness of my womanhood. After all, it's not every day you get more than one use out of a wedding dress!

A month or two later in August, my husband and I had gone on a double date to the state fair when we bumped into Toy. She told me she'd confirmed the specifics for the photoshoot as soon as the final details were complete. I did not mind because this was an opportunity to live out one of my childhood dreams of modeling. Chrisette knew this.

DATING DADDY

On our way home from the fair, I overheard my husband say he wanted to try the HandleBar, a popular activity where sixteen people pedal a trolley-like vehicle around downtown Indianapolis while consuming beer and wine. My ears perked up as this sounded like something he really wanted to do, and I made a mental note to plan a HandleBar for his thirtieth birthday the following month. I wanted to surprise him.

But planning this was not easy. What started off as a guys-only surprise party became a mixed-gender gathering that included some of my friends to fill the HandleBar. One of Deion's friends waited until the last possible moment to RSVP because he did not believe the party would go on. I had gotten extremely angry with him because I thought he was one of Deion's best friends, yet he was on the fence about committing to the birthday plans. Was this a sign?

Around this time, our marriage was going through a rocky period. We had been growing apart. I could feel the distance since spring and when I had approached him about it, he brushed it off. Now, a few months later, he seemed to be echoing the same sentiments I had shared with him earlier. Deion initiated several conversations regarding the status of our marriage.

Part of me was glad he was vocal about his concerns because he had seemed closed off to me for months. Any time I wanted to share things with him, he had seemed distracted. After a while, the more he pushed me away, the more I sought help for our marriage outside the home. I even resumed a focus on my spiritual growth by visiting a new church. But after months of being pushed away, I had finally reached the point of frustration and lost the desire to work on our marriage. Deion could sense this. He had to know that I was slowly giving up because I was no longer present when we were together.

He began asking me if someone else had my attention. I

INTRODUCTION

had noticed that when I would take a shower or nap, I'd find him pretending to take a selfie with my phone to cover up the fact that he was actually investigating its contents. Instead of answering his question directly with yes or no, I told him he had been pushing me away for so long that it was becoming easier for others to have my attention. But why did he even care? If our marriage mattered to him, why didn't he try to maintain our relationship instead of snooping around to see if I was being unfaithful? Anyone who knew me could see I was madly in love with Deion and would do anything for him. But this rough season of our marriage was starting to take a toll on me.

On the weekend of Deion's thirtieth birthday, any feelings of hopelessness in our marriage had been subsided by my desperate attempt to plan the best surprise birthday weekend for him. I just knew it would be a weekend he would never forget! I thought he would love the surprise and maybe it would help close the gap in our distant connection. Instead, it would become a weekend *neither* of us would ever forget—even if we had wanted to.

The Friday of his birthday weekend, Deion had hung out with his friends. This gave me time to plan my shopping trip to purchase the beer and wine for the HandleBar and other last-minute details for Sunday night. Everything was going to be perfect! But what was expected to be the joyous event that would bring us back together became something horribly different.

It all began Saturday night following our private pre-birthday dinner. Words were said. The effect of which would push us in different rooms of our apartment for the night. Deion asked me to cancel whatever plan I had for Sunday, but I told him there was too much involved to do so.

Sunday…well, we'll talk about that later.

By Monday morning, I sat puffy-eyed and sick, the effects of a hangover and a severe migraine induced by all the tears I had cried. I crouched in a small space on our large L-shaped couch, alone, sobbing and wondering if Deion was ever coming home again.

Were we really getting a divorce???

***

Just a week or two after Deion's departure, Toy had reached out to me to confirm the details for the bridal photoshoot. I had called Chrisette in tears.

"Chrisette, I cannot do this!"

She listened attentively.

"How do I do this wedding-inspired photoshoot when my marriage is falling apart?"

I deeply feared that once I looked back at these beautiful pictures, they would remind me of the broken state of my own marriage. Though she is known for her intrepid personality, Chrisette listened quietly as I shared my uncertainty about the photoshoot. After a long pause, Chrisette said in the softest voice I had ever heard her speak, "You should do this for you."

I didn't understand her in that moment, but I trusted what she had to say even if I could not believe it for myself, and decided I would say yes. The next two weeks leading up to the photoshoot, however, I plotted all the excuses I could use to get out of it.

I had an unexpected commitment come up.

Oops, I didn't wake up on time.

And the best and most honest reason of them all…

My husband left.

But in the back of my mind, I could hear Chrisette: "This will be good for you." For the life of me, I could not see *any* good of doing a wedding shoot in my wedding gown and pretending to be happily married! Let's face it, I was absolutely miserable and extremely fragile to the point of crying a river at any moment. Meanwhile, my husband was sleeping somewhere else with no sign of coming back. In the midst of my indecisiveness, it was Chrisette's tender voice that scooted me toward the photoshoot even through my toddler-like reluctance.

Prepping for the actual shoot felt like wading through a thick layer of mire. I gathered several items including my hygiene bag and tulle slip and placed them in my gym bag. Then I grabbed the item that quickened the floodgates from my eyes: my wedding dress. The tears were uncontrollable and I ceased all movement in my body. I held on and rode out the emotional wave, hung the garment bag containing my beautiful gown in the living room, and retired to our king-sized bed, alone.

The day of the shoot, I resolved not to speak a word about my marriage to anyone, including the makeup artist whom I knew personally. During our conversation in which I sat captive in her chair, I was able to indirectly answer her questions and avoid a total breakdown. After makeup, I changed into my gown and was one of the first of three models to have her photos taken indoors.

When the indoor shoot wrapped, I accepted their offer to take additional photos in a beautiful park nearby. The photos from the outdoor location turned out to be some of the most riveting of the entire shoot. Even in my anguish, everything about that day made me feel more beautiful than I had felt on my actual wedding day. But because the reality of my marriage was grim, I questioned the missteps of my journey that led to this point. How had I gotten here? A beautiful bride with a soft flowing veil, a fresh bouquet of roses, and alone... This would begin the process of searching for answers that would take me all the way back to my childhood.

JEHOVAH-JIREH
My Provider

Shavonne in October 1984 at three months old.

CHAPTER 1

OUR FATHER, WHICH ART IN HEAVEN...

ON-TIME GOD

"THANK YOU, JESUS! THANK YOU, Jesus! Thank you, Jesus! Thank you, Jesus! Thank you, JESUS!" Mom'ela, as I affectionately call my mother, would say this as fast as a cheetah in the wild any time a utility bill was paid before the disconnection date. "Thank you, Jesus" the day before a big holiday and we were gifted enough groceries for a sufficient meal. "Thank you, Jesus" for all the other breakthroughs that happened in the nick of time.

As a child, I came to know God as an "on-time" God through these and other miracles He performed. God was like an imaginary friend, always floating so high in the sky that my mother had to look up when she thanked Him. He was who we thanked for blessing us with a meal, even though Mom'ela prepared the food. Whenever she found herself in a corner faced with a major decision, she would say, "God will take care of us." It was as if He was just responding to crises when I was taught that He had the power to keep us from experiencing distress or discomfort in the first place.

We lived in a constant state of lack as my mother struggled to raise us two children on her own. My father wasn't actively involved in my upbringing. In my opinion, mothers and fathers each have distinct purposes in a child's life. Between my mother and father, Mom'ela's influence molded me the greatest. She tried to process her own life, childhood hang-ups, and shortcomings, all while trying to take care of me and my sister—which made for one rocky ride.

As a child, I realized Mom'ela often felt alone and had a longing in her heart for unconditional love. She was the seventh of nine children on her mother's side and had five siblings on her father's side. Also raised by her mother, Mom'ela often called herself the "black sheep" of the family because she felt like an outsider amongst her siblings and had a darker complexion than many of her brothers and sisters. She hoped that her children would give her the love she longed for.

I am my mother's oldest child and my sister was born two years and nine months later. Though we have different fathers, I never considered her my half-sister because she was all I knew. My first name comes from my maternal grandmother, Yvonne, who was pursued by a man who could not say her name correctly, adding the "sh" to the beginning. Oddly, I don't think my mother or grandmother realized the significance of my name. In college, I looked up its meaning and found it derives from the Irish name "Siobhan," which means "God is gracious."

As a single mother, Mom'ela had a difficult time ensuring we had everything we needed. We relied on government assistance and charities to provide our basic needs. Our clothes were often hand-me-down items from our cousin who was two years older than me; when she could not fit her clothes, they would be given to me and then passed to my sister once I grew out of them. My sister and I received free and reduced meals from school and this guaranteed at least breakfast and lunch each day.

By the time I was nine years old, I realized my mother was addicted to drugs, and the embarrassment of this affected my interactions with other kids. I carried the shame from my life at home to the classroom at school. I tried to avoid unnecessary conversations that would reveal what I had been hiding from my teachers, peers, and neighbors. At school, my peers had newer clothes, shoes, and cash for lunch items or supplies from the bookstore. My sister and I did not. Our cleanest look appeared disheveled next to our peers. In our neighborhood, my sister and I were often teased by the bullies, and even with our friends we became targets when the opportunity served them. No matter where I turned, I felt as if I did not have friends. My only friends were my sister and cousins.

LATE NIGHT (SPIRITUAL) RENDEZVOUS

Meanwhile, Mom'ela's friends were typically other drug addicts who spent considerable amounts of time in our home. Anyone who visited was required to contribute to the needs of our household. It was like their admissions fee for occupying our space to indulge in their habits. Admissions included meals, cash, or whatever else Mom'ela requested. Day or night, Mom'ela ran errands to ensure our needs were met. Other times, she'd leave home to chase the next high.

On one such evening, she returned home and asked my sister and me if we wanted to be baptized with her. I didn't fully understand her, but I was all ears! She explained that she met a minister while she was out and he would perform our baptism at a church located one block away from the apartments we lived in.

Within moments, we were walking to the small church that was no bigger than a cozy ranch-sized home and were led to a small room containing the tub in which the baptisms were performed. The minister explained something, presumably about salvation, before my mother and I were baptized. That evening, I was hopeful for the first time. I believed my mother would change and that this was a new beginning for our family. At the age of nine, that experience marked the beginning of my journey with God.

The following Sunday, I began to attend that little apostolic church religiously and my sister willingly went along for the ride. I was consumed by the church and its ideals of who God was, evidence of the Holy Spirit, and anything gleaned from the many services we attended throughout the week. When the church doors were open, I was there with my sister in tow. One of the deacons and his wife served as our surrogate parents and ensured we had what we needed outside of service times.

At home, Mom'ela returned to life as usual with her drug habit and frequent traffic in our home. The last time she had maintained a full-time job, I was molested by our babysitter's adult son. So, bound by the guilt of someone violating her baby girl, she had resolved to stay home to care for us. I was molested before I became of school age, but now I was in the fifth grade and she had not maintained a job for quite some time.

It was no secret what was going on in our home because our neighbors and their kids knew. We were often teased by other kids, who had overheard their parents saying things about our mother and her addiction. How could these kids talk about my family when they were growing up in the same horrible neighborhood as us? Even some of their parents were using drugs with my mom! In the midst of all this chaos and my growing emotional insecurities, the church became my safe place.

It was at church where I began to see God as my refuge. God gave me joy as I sang the hymns I memorized during moments of despair. I truly believed that "There's not a friend like the lowly Jesus" and "There is power, power, wond'rous working power in the blood of the lamb." As I focused on these hymns, I went from feeling helpless to hopeful that things would get better someday.

DISTANT LOVE

As I transitioned to my pre-adolescent years, Mom'ela began to feel threatened by the church because she believed they were brainwashing us. My pastor openly petitioned prayer requests on behalf of our family during the Sunday morning service. Once she became aware of this, she set limits for the time we could spend at church until eventually it evolved into us leaving the church altogether. She had to have known how much I loved going to church because I asked her to go every time there was a service. So when she limited how much I could go, I felt she was keeping me from the only thing that gave me joy.

By sixth grade, feelings of shame continued due to my mother's drug addiction, and this made the transition to middle school difficult. I did not seek out new friendships and found ways to isolate myself in such a large school. My hair was short because my mother chopped it off as a punishment for trimming my sister's hair—which my mom had asked me to do. She later admitted she was probably under the influence of drugs, but the damage was done. What little self-esteem I had was shattered.

By second semester of sixth grade, I didn't feel God's protection. Like the story of Job, God allowed us to experience a whirlwind of events that shook our foundation. In January 1996, Mom'ela lost a brother on her father's side and another brother on her mother's side within a day of each other. If I thought my mom had a drug habit before, I didn't know how bad it could get: the loss of her brothers quickly set in motion Mom's downward spiral to full-on abuse as she tried to cope with loss. Our already unstable foundation fell apart as we lost our home and began our lives as transients.

When I was in seventh grade, our family of three lived in at least two different homeless shelters, a shack, and spent nights in a car parked in a mechanic's garage. Somewhere during the various transitions, my sister and I spent nights with family members before being taken away by Child Protective Services and placed in the foster care system. I missed my mother yet I was tired of living such an unstable life. Unable to process the complexity of my emotions, I attempted to take my own life while in the care of our first foster parent. At twelve years old, I believed life with God in heaven would be better than the hell I was experiencing on earth. Why couldn't I be with my mother? Why couldn't she stop using drugs? I felt utterly alone during this time.

One year and two foster homes later, my mother gained full custody of us. By that time, I was in eighth grade. Mom'ela established a more stable living environment and was actively working the Twelve-Step program. Once we were reunited, we began visiting a new church where "Jesus is exalted and the Word is explained." The pastor delivered charismatic sermons that made the Bible more practical for everyday living. Until this point, the Word of God seemed out of touch and outdated, but this pastor made the supernatural relevant by ministering to the middle. Everyone from the college educated professional to the person who spent much of their life on the streets understood what the pastor preached. Each sermon or message made biblical concepts more tangible and applicable to everyday life.

This church was located across the street from the school I attended and they were gracious enough to host our school's eighth grade graduation ceremony. To me, the ceremony symbolized both the closing of a dark chapter in my life and the commencement of a more hope-filled one.

CLOSE BY ASSOCIATION

By the time I went to high school, my faith in God's existence lay dormant within me. At the core of my being, I believed in Him but life had shaken me to the point that I did not actively seek a relationship with Him like I once had in elementary school. Even though I could not sense His presence, God still ordered my steps and positioned me in environments that would nourish me spiritually.

As iron sharpens iron, so a man sharpens the countenance of his friend.
~Proverbs 27:17

Like anything that lies dormant, my relationship with God would soon be reignited by something that activated it from within. In high school, a divine camaraderie of four ladies would spark my passion for God. Each of these ladies had a relationship with God that I admired. Riley was the daughter of a pastor and she maintained a visible presence in their small church. What I admire most about her is her ability to communicate with depth and her quest for making meaning of life.

Similarly, the second girl, Chrisette, had parents whose faith was evident to all who knew them. She proclaimed bold statements in Christ much like her mother, who has the gift of prophesy.

Their family would have the most consistent influence in my life as well as the life of the third girl, Dior Chante, who was considered their adopted daughter. I had met Dior Chante in sixth or seventh grade and learned we had similar backgrounds filled with instability that now fueled our ambitions for a better life.

I would meet the fourth girl, Kamille, during sophomore year; she was rooted in the church as well. She has the biggest heart and is one of the most resourceful people I know. Kamille remembers birthdays, gives gifts "just because," and sends cards for almost every life event.

And then there was me. The girl who met God in elementary school and held on to Him with all her might, but did not have a personal relationship with Him that was remotely close to what her new friends had. Each of us behaved like typical teenagers and our shared interest in pursuing a career in health care is what brought us together in high school. But it was beyond the classroom where they most impacted my spiritual walk.

Over the years, our friendship included both laughter and joy as well as opportunities to develop each other in love. I was not a big fan of confrontation. Yet, our group held what would become known as "interventions" to address issues that other group members were not willing to face. These interventions would happen during a girls' night in with snacks. Sometimes it would end with us laughing, and other times the issues were too complex for them to be resolved in one night.

During these interventions, the feedback I often received was about my strength and how it kept me guarded even within the safety of the group. Nothing could have been further from the truth. I trusted these ladies. They believed in the same God I came to know and they were open about their relationship with Him. God seemed to be an ever-present part of their experience. Yet I had lived much of my life with an understanding of God as my distant Heavenly Father and our relationship was estranged. God the Father, as I had come to know Him, was a rolling stone. He would be a part of my life during one season and out the next.

For the first time in a long time, though, I began to trust God through these friends, and these ladies would continue to challenge me throughout my budding spiritual journey. I was challenged to pray more, even if it was just a little, and to seek His guidance in the issues I had at home. By the end of high school, God and I were getting to know each other again. Through the examples of these amazing young women, God showed me new possibilities for my future. I saw what a healthy relationship looks like. I felt what iron sharpening iron meant. To this day, my friendship with these ladies challenges me to keep growing spiritually.

As I reflect on the events of my childhood, it was evident who the key players were in my spiritual development. My mother, church, and friends oriented me to God, but I had challenges understanding Him for myself. "Our Father which art in Heaven" (Matthew 6:9-13) really felt that way to me: in heaven, distant, and inaccessible much like my earthly father. His presence in my life was not consistent, which caused me to have periods where I questioned His love for me and, at times, His existence. How could God be so loving if He allowed me to experience and to witness all that I endured as a child? Why didn't He make more of an effort to protect his daughter?

CHAPTER 2

FATHER(S) FOR THE FATHERLESS

I cannot think of any need in childhood as strong as the need for a father's protection.
~Sigmund Freud

I HAVE FORGIVEN MY DAD as much as I know how to for his absence. Yet, it is easy for me to imagine how different my experiences would have been had he been more involved in my upbringing. I've known friends who grew up in two-parent households but had fathers who were unavailable emotionally or physically for various reasons. While I cannot speak for them, I believe I would not have gone through some of the trials I faced had he protected me. As a result, I had to make mature decisions that ate away at my childhood innocence.

UNCOVERED

What I needed most from my dad was protection. I needed him to protect me from the things my young mind could not comprehend. Without him, I assumed responsibility for issues beyond my control, including the need to support my family in the midst of my mother's drug addiction.

Even if you overlooked the costs associated with a chemical dependence, it is not uncommon for single mothers to experience financial hardships as they adjust to their new normal. Journalist Victoria Secunda has studied extensively the father-daughter relationship. In her book, *Women and Their Fathers: The Sexual and Romantic Impact of the First Man of Your Life*, she notes that it is common for a mother to recover from a divorce (or breakup) by downsizing her living spaces and "her children may have to start over in new schools and neighborhoods...fending for themselves."

But downsizing in my family was not what you might imagine it to be. In such a short time, we went from living in a duplex where each of us dozed off in our own beds at night to sleeping inside one car in a mechanics shop, and sometimes we were allowed to sleep in the mechanic shop owner's shack.

Simply put—I hated this! I was tired of picking up our belongings on a whim and moving to a new place after a day or two. So much so that I began imagining ways I could run away from it all. One night, I worked up the courage to live out this fantasy and escaped in the middle of the night. My attempt was an absolute fail! When I returned to the shack, I was welcomed by my worried mom who said she had been looking for me for some time. I was too afraid and could not explain why I left in the middle of the night—and then it happened. I had been disciplined before, but this time my mother's hand came across my face faster than I could blink. She "burst" my bubble quicker than the pop of a balloon, leaving me with a visible blood clot in one eye.

As a pre-teen, I learned I should not get comfortable at any particular school because the moment I did, we moved. Our moves were not from one neighborhood to another. It was more like from one unstable environment to the next shaky situation until we were taken away from our mother.

Each time we returned to Mom, I was already conditioned to believe life would always be unstable and to change it, I had to advocate for both my sister and myself. I eagerly awaited the day I could work and have my own cash to rely on.

My first part-time job was in fast food and I had to catch two city buses to get to work each shift. Imagine the challenges of being a student athlete who spent three hours traveling round trip for a part-time job. I was often drained, but I was also excited to finally make my own money that no one could touch—or so I thought. Every weekend, I deposited each check I received in the bank to ensure my sister and I had emergency funds. Because I was a minor, Mom had to cosign on the account, which also meant she had access to the funds. At first, I noticed small amounts of money disappearing from the account here and there. Once I realized she was making regular withdrawals, I started keeping cash on me, hidden at home, or with my best friend from the basketball team.

When I think about the ways I needed and wanted my father's help and protection, financial resources was not really one of them. In fact, I believe his way of protecting me could have been as simple as giving me a safe place as an alternative to the environment I grew up in. Though family members provided a rescue every now and then, ultimately, I felt the weight of our household on my shoulders. At a time when other teenagers worked for discretionary income, I worked because our family of three had real needs that my mother could not manage and my father was most likely oblivious to.

A HOLY PROTECTION

Since Dad did not protect me, I turned to things outside of the home. School and family both provided a meaningful outlet, but my true sanctuary was found in the church. The church protected me by providing a place to clear my mind. I'd approach the services carrying the burdens of poverty, shame, and uncertainty, but I was able to put down my baggage at the door. My mind may have been filled with worries about our next meal or new clothes for school, but coming to the house of God provided temporary relief from it all. If I could have lived in the church, I would have done so happily.

The impact of the apostolic church followed my sister and me as we hosted our own services at home. In our shared bedroom, we had one of the old-school twenty-four-inch tube televisions on a blue milk crate. The tube of the TV served as a podium and the antennas were our microphones. We had full church services with selections from the "choir" while my sister and I alternated preaching the sermon. She was much better at mimicking our pastor's delivery style while my strength lay in biblical knowledge. My sister and I look back on these memories and laugh. But this type of play helped to take my mind off our reality and experience a peace similar to what we experienced in the actual church services.

Our church attendance significantly decreased in middle school, but I continued to feel close with God through music. Music has and continues to give me the most intimate feeling with Him. It is through singing hymns and gospel music that I feel closer to God than I ever did in prayer. When I was introduced to Kirk Franklin and all the mass choirs in middle school, my infatuation with gospel music reached a new level. I loved the depth and layers in the music, reminiscent of the hymnals from the church of my youth, with a contemporary sound.

While attending the 21st Century Scholarship camp the summer between middle and high school, I met Riley. She was a quiet, dark-haired, innocent girl with cheeks like Kerry Washington. Every day, we took a music break to sing this one gospel song that our other new friend taught us earlier that week. Every time our little camp gospel choir sang in three-part harmony, I could feel the presence of God amongst us. It was so surreal.

Unbeknownst to me at the time, my Heavenly Father had his hand of protection over me. I would come to understand that what I learned in the house of God protected my mind while at home and out in the world when my father could not. Whether it was playing church with my sister or learning contemporary gospel music in foster care, I believe that God was using these things to cover me. He knew what I needed when I did not. It was as if He set up provisions for me, knowing what I would face in life. This meant I always could fall back on scriptures and songs when faced with life's challenges. I had holy tools in my kit.

On the other hand, church also allowed me to mask the pain I did not face head-on. I now realize I underestimated the importance of mental health, concluding that my dad's absence did not affect me. For most of my life, I believed I was okay because I survived growing up in poverty and made it to college. Isn't that what it means to be successful? Unfortunately, in the process I was sweeping critical issues that bothered me under the rug and kept pressing on. In my way of thinking, each day I overcame the obstacles of life served as evidence of my strength. In the process, I accepted some dysfunctional behavior and false convictions as reality, to my own detriment.

MISPERCEPTION OF DADDY'S ABSENCE

One toxic belief I long held was that my father was absent because he did not love me. That he did not care enough about me to fight for a place in my life. However, I have come to know that there are many reasons for a father's departure from his child's life. My father's absence was more complicated than I could imagine as a young child. What I will say is I couldn't imagine the struggle he had to go through to choose to not be a part of my life.

For some daughters, the ending of a life chapter can create a chasm between a daughter and her daddy. It could be the death of the relationship with the mother where the damage between the parents makes it nearly impossible to co-parent.

Another possibility is in the unfortunate event of the father's passing while the child is yet too young to comprehend death or loss. Still there are deadbeat or distant fathers who remain in the home but do not engage their families. Whatever the cause for the father's absence or distance, the lack of meaningful attachment with his daughter can negatively impact her future romantic relationships.

> "Whatever the cause for the father's absence or distance, the lack of meaningful attachment with his daughter can negatively impact her future romantic relationships."

Psychoanalysts like Sigmund Freud have long studied effects of attachment and loss. Freud's findings were focused mainly on the attachment and loss between a mother and her child. By the 1930's, British psychiatrist John Bowlby's seminal work expounded upon Freud's theories to explain the effects of attachment and loss more broadly. According to Bowlby, attachments are created when you gravitate toward someone who you feel is more competent in handling a crisis. You believe they have it all together more than you. However, when that attachment is severed, there are serious emotional consequences.

For the longest time, I wanted to be near my dad because it would be an escape from my reality. He seemed to have made it out and thrived. As a result, I dated some men who symbolized this very thing—men who had successfully made it despite the odds against them. In my own experience, Bowlby's theory appeared to be true because when those relationships ended, I experienced varying degrees of anxiety.

Another common belief is that a father's absence creates irreparable damage to the daughter's well-being. In a study to understand the effects of a father's engagement, developmental psychologist Rebekah Coley analyzed 302 African-American teens and noted their tendency to isolate themselves or act out in school. The study found that the girls who had minimum interactions with their father tended to alienate or disengage in school and misbehave more than those who had higher quality interactions with their biological or other father figures. What resonated with me was in Coley's interpretation of the data. She stated that girls, among other factors, "could simply interpret their relationships with their fathers in a negative manner," which prompted me to take personal inventory. Had I misunderstood my father's departure as a lack of love?

> *Because I delivered the poor who cried out, the fatherless and the one who had no helper.*
> ~Job 29:12

On her blog post *Healing the Father Daughter Relationship*, Sarah Best writes, "Girls will mistake their fathers' issues for their own—if their father doesn't relate to them with love, they'll assume they must therefore not be loveable." Because our parents, or fathers in particular, are trying to navigate the issues of life while raising us, they can transfer those issues onto their children if they do not know how to handle them properly. As children, we may feel unlovable even when our father's issues have absolutely nothing to do with us. As we grow and mature and face struggles of our own, we develop empathy for our parents—and a better understanding of ourselves in the process.

IT TAKES A VILLAGE

At first glance, it would appear this scripture in Job 29:12 was spoken by God, but it was actually a narrative from Job. In his distress, he was recounting the ways in which he had done charitable deeds in the world—not in a boastful manner, but to recall the days he had lived under the favor of God. He had gone through so much in the first twenty-nine chapters of the book that he needed some semblance of hope—at least, that is my understanding of it.

After reading this scripture, I was reminded of the other men who played father-like roles during my upbringing. It's much easier to point the finger at my dad for his absence, or to say that I turned out to be such a bad person because he neglected me. But that would negate the men whom God placed in our lives as surrogate fathers. Like Job, there were men who played a supportive role to my family during our seasons of despair. Men who were either related to me or in the community who helped me build a positive self-identity. God constantly surrounded me with men who sowed words of encouragement and affirmation, met the basic needs of our household, introduced me to God, and who modeled manhood while teaching me the expectations I needed to set for my future relationships. I will highlight some of the positive male role models throughout the book.

One of my childhood mentors inspired me to set high goals and to focus on developing my character and use it as the foundation for my choices. He is the president of a non-for-profit organization that empowers minority youth in Indianapolis through various programs. He was probably the first Black lawyer I had ever encountered and continues to be a well-respected individual in the community. I was always fascinated with his eloquent delivery of words. He spoke intentionally and with great purpose like any Black character from the family sitcoms of the 1980s and 1990s. His name is Mr. Dennis Bland and he co-facilitated the Self-Discovery/Career Exploration class I participated in during my last semester of high school.

Each week, for thirteen weeks, I left the class in a better mood than when I arrived. It was evident that Mr. Bland believed in all the students who participated. He found moments to inquire on each student's well-being. Though there were approximately twenty students in my class, each one was made to feel important and worthwhile. Unlike teachers in school, he did not hide his faith in God. Most important, Mr. Bland's passion for empowering minority youth imbued my desire to give back to the community.

The support he and the organization provided extended beyond that initial self-discovery program. In its early days, the organization started with a few programs that primarily targeted high school aged youth. By the time I participated, the organization grew and now it is serving younger-aged students with even more opportunities for personal growth and professional exposure.

Regardless of the number of initiatives the center maintains, any time I needed moral support throughout college, I could call up my mentor and set up a meeting to talk things through. For instance, I struggled with the idea of taking out student loans once my scholarship money ran low. When I met with Mr. Bland, he shared the importance of investing in education and that some investments require sacrifice. Because I invested in my education, I am able to write this book as a first-generation college graduate with a master's degree! He has made such a lasting impact that I have returned to the center as a regular volunteer.

My respect for Mr. Bland and his contributions have grown significantly now that I have a career in higher education. Our professional spheres have now coalesced and I have had the privilege of witnessing him being honored for his work and am now compelled to leave a similar legacy of my own.

As I explored the effects of absent fathers on daughters, I am grateful to God for the earthly surrogates He has placed along my path. Men like Mr. Bland have instilled in me strong values through their active involvement in my life. At times when I could have succumbed to negative peer pressure, I felt more compelled to take the positive route. Maybe I was a responsible child, but it was most likely due to the guilt I would have felt from letting anyone of my "fathers" down.

CHAPTER 3

MAKING MEANING OF GOD, THE PROVIDER

*The issue of father absence then becomes more a matter
of daughter's interpretation of the experience and much less
a matter of what fathers do or don't do.*
~Dr. Eunice Matthews-Armstead, Clinical Social Worker/Therapist

FROM KINDERGARTEN THROUGH HIGH SCHOOL, it is evident that God was present even before I truly understood it. My earliest comprehension of Him was as a provider and the church as a safe place. A shared belief in God is what bonded me with the lifelong friends I met in high school. A strong spiritual foundation was the common thread shared by the men who had the most significant impact in my development. Whether directly or indirectly, I learned many valuable lessons throughout the earlier part of my life.

GOD BLESSES THROUGH RELATIONSHIPS

God's work is not always logical to us. He will place people in our lives for a particular purpose for a season. God's provisions come to us how He wants them to come. His provisions will also come from whomever He wants them to come from. He will sometimes use the least likely person who barely knows your history to bless you. When we think about raising children, we expect two parents in the home to provide positive guidance, but that is not always reality.

Sometimes God provides us with the positive influence of others outside of the home who sow into our well-being in ways that our parents cannot. We must appreciate those who are in our lives instead of focusing on the people who are missing. There are mentors and teachers who will go to great lengths for us because they believe in us. They believe in our dreams. They see something within us that we are unable to see in ourselves.

Mr. Bland saw my potential even when I lacked the vision to see beyond my present circumstances. I aspired to go to college but did not have the foresight or guidance to know my next steps in achieving this goal. Mr. Bland was one of the most significant influences in my life who intentionally nurtured my development and provided moral support when I went to college. I feel this kind of support, sadly, is becoming less common among the current generation.

We live in a time where we undervalue the lessons our elders can teach us. They have experienced love and loss time and time again. On the surface, their experiences may appear drastically different than ours, but the emotions on life's rollercoaster is a shared experience that expands across generations. We all know the feeling of desperation when pursuing the thing or opportunity we've longed for. We know the hopelessness of facing roadblock after never-ending roadblock. Times and technology may change but emotional experiences do not.

Another point about relationships is that most often the people who have our best interest at heart are those who adopt us into their family. I have had the support of my family, but they were not always present for the everyday struggles I experienced. They had their own lives to live and obligations to maintain. My mom's maternal siblings, in particular, struggled to change our family dynamics while battling their own private demons. Some family members fought hard to avoid poverty by overworking while others drowned their tears in drugs or alcohol.

When my family was unavailable or grew weary in their efforts to support us, I learned to appreciate the people who were there with us in the trenches. My friends' parents instilled in me values that I did not learn from home. I learned many lessons from the hours spent in their homes. My first church family nurtured the initial steps of my spiritual journey. Not only did we have surrogate parents in the church, but the pastor's teenage children became our big brothers and sisters as well. Each and every person who has sown positively into my life entered at the appropriate time. I am fortunate to be one of the last generations where the community truly looked out for its children without the fears of violence and exploitation we now face. I experienced firsthand the saying, "It takes a village to raise a child."

Society projects two-parent households as the standard for a happy life, but many of us come from broken homes with or without our biological parents. Instead, we must learn to appreciate those who join us in our journey instead of relying on preconceived notions of the makings of a "healthy" family. Had I focused on all that I did not have, I would have placed too much focus into meaningless expectations and missed out on the blessings in front of me.

At the same time, we must extend grace to those who do not love us in the way we would have preferred—especially our fathers. Maybe they did not know we needed a hug to calm our anxieties. Dad may not have known we needed to be affirmed by his presence or with his words, because he was not affirmed as a child. So when others come into our lives and nourish us in the ways that we desire, we cannot minimize their role in feeding our spirits nor should we resent our fathers for their lack of know-how. We all inherit ways of loving that are flawed and unintentionally pass them on in some form if we do not become aware.

DATING DADDY

WHAT'S SWEPT UNDER THE RUG ISN'T CLEAN

In childhood, you are given permission to feel everything and let others know about your feelings freely. When you were an infant, for instance, your parents knew your hunger cry. They knew your screams meant your Pampers or diapers were soiled from the last meal you ingested. When you were a toddler, the adults in your life knew you were fatigued by either your hyperactivity or the way you rubbed your eyes wearily. Once you were of school age, your parents were aware that you were up to something mischievous once they heard the shift from audible laughter to absolute silence in the next room.

No matter what caused you to respond in pleasure, discontent, or rage, the adults in your life excused your behavior because you were a child who was yet learning the appropriate way to make your needs known. All you knew was that you had these impulses within that caused you to react in a particular way and it was up to your caregivers to set the guidelines for your behavior.

But somewhere along the way, we are told not to respond to situations that naturally produce a reaction. We are hushed in the quiet rooms of museums when we see our first nude sculpture. We are silenced in sanctuaries when we notice a lady's slip hanging longer than her dress and try to tell our parent of our discovery. Some of us are reprimanded for crying too much if we are being bullied in school and are unable to fight back. These redirections inadvertently teach us to keep a lid on our feelings and the truth of our experiences.

And for those of us who have absent fathers, we're told to stop crying when they do not show up as promised. We're told our father is away on a long business trip when he is actually deceased. The lies to cover up daddy's other woman, or even his entire other family, are told to protect both our hearts and our mothers' who were left behind. The lies will continue for as long as they can hold up, until finally we learn to ignore our true feelings inside and wear the mask of being unaffected.

I did not experience all the aforementioned; however, for a long time I did believe the lie that I was okay without my father. From the strong women in my life, I repeatedly heard the message that I too must be strong and press on WITH or WITHOUT a man. In a way, they minimized the importance of the interconnectedness of woman and man. I was learning to undervalue what men could contribute to our lives and did not see the value of having a healthy romantic relationship.

> *"I too must be strong and press on WITH or WITHOUT a man."*

The lies that are told to us can be damaging if we continue to ignore them and do not address them head-on. My friends know me to be an optimistic person, but part of my positive disposition was that I often overlooked the things that bothered me. I did not give much energy to things others considered problems because I had overcome "worse" issues that made everything else appear minor. In my mind, I minimized others' good news to ease my feelings of deficiency. In my spirit, I believed everything would turn out favorably in the long run with or without my father. What I came to know is that the issues we sweep under the rug do not go away; they are still in the crevices of the floorboards of our hearts, collecting dust while continuing to subtly or not so subtly influence all our decisions.

What does this mean? It means it is not okay to pretend we do not need our fathers. It means we must be open to a father's demonstration of love and care even if it is not the way we prefer to receive it. Hear me: I am not saying to accept abuse or maltreatment of any kind. But we cannot ignore the value of the men in our lives or the unrest created by their absence. We need to allow children to express their hurt in healthy ways instead of overlooking it. Most important, as adults who may have had an absent father, we need to give ourselves permission to grieve them. If we do not, we may enter romantic relationships that are not fruitful because we have not done the work. We must acknowledge the truth about our biological father's absence and face it head-on.

GOD'S DELAY IS NOT A DENIAL

For as long as I can remember, I learned to turn to God for everything. Not only did I witness Mom'ela's praise and gratitude when God made a way for us to persist through our problems, but GMa often repeated that "All you have in the world is God." She would say my mother, her own daughter, would let me down, but as long as I have God I would have all that I needed.

GMa poured so much into me that I felt like one of her children and her lessons were well received. Not only was I named after her, but in her I felt the deep connection I wanted from my mother. I thought that all I had in the world was God, GMa, and myself. No family member was safe from her verbal lashings, though. GMa would berate all her children, including my mother! At first, I excused GMa's mood switch as a random episode of purging her own pent up anger. However, I came to realize that it was a part of her personality and learned the signs of her "bait them then berate them" transition in conversations. When GMa turned on me, I was promptly reminded of her original lesson that all I have in the world was God. Got it!

Almost anyone who has memorized a verse of scripture has heard of Psalm 27:10 and understands that God will be with us especially when our mothers or fathers desert us. Our parents can desert us in many ways including physically, emotionally, and spiritually. Physical desertion is obvious, but our parents can abandon us emotionally when we are unable to connect with them, whether they are physically available or not. Spiritually, there may be dissonance if a child seeks a relationship with God and isn't able to see that relationship modeled by her parents. For me, Mom'ela exerted her power and influence to limit how frequently I could attend church.

Not only did I feel deserted by my father during my childhood, but there were also times I felt deserted by my mother. Her chemical dependency consumed her to the point of neglecting us. When she was sober, we had the best of times and had the strongest of connections. But when she returned to using, I felt that we lost her. After so many cycles of this, I was tired of trying to forge a relationship with her. I felt alone and learned to become my own advocate while seeking a better life for myself.

Though I felt deserted by both parents, God was constant. I could see traces of Him as He made provisions for my sister and me. No matter how desperately I yearned to have some stability for us, I can truly say we never made it to the last possible resource. There was always a miracle right around the corner if we held on.

It may have felt that He ignored us because God's timing was never in sync with our deadlines or in tandem with the way we expected things to happen. For instance, I expected our parents to supply us with school clothes and supplies when the list was distributed weeks before the start of fall semester. Every fall, we would come up short on the supplies needed for school, but in the nick of time family members and people in the community would provide everything we needed. My sister and I went to school on the first day with new clothes and shoes, but they did not always come from our parents. God blessed us with a village of family, community members, and the church to stand in when our parents did not. He spoke to the hearts of those who "randomly" thought about us and dropped off what we needed, on time and not a moment sooner.

God's timing reminds me of the story of Lazarus in John 11. In the story, Jesus arrived at Lazarus's tomb long after all signs of life had left him and there was great doubt that his body could be revived naturally. But God gave life to what appeared to be a dead situation. Similarly, I learned to trust God to deliver us through the periods that seemed impossible to overcome. When it appeared that we would not have a meal on Thanksgiving, He provided food. When homelessness seemed a certainty, He made our living conditions more stable. When I longed for a relationship with my biological father, God used some wonderful men to model and stand in for him. God always blessed us, but it was never in the way or the timing I expected it to be.

In fact, He would answer my long-awaited, heart-felt prayer but not in the way I expected. More than anything, I wanted my dad to be a part of my childhood, and he was periodically, but our deepest connection happened after high school and at a time when I believed it was too late for my dad to even connect with me. I thought he had already missed all the important years and milestones. But as you have gleaned from my story thus far and possibly from your own experience, God does not work according to our clocks and deadlines. He works according to His divine timing.

DAD:
Model of Manhood

Shavonne attended IPS Booth Tarkington Elementary School #92.
Pictured here in second grade.

CHAPTER 4

HONORING AN ABSENT FATHER

Honor your father and your mother that your days may be long upon the land which the Lord your God is giving you.
~Exodus 20:12

HOW DO YOU HONOR SOMEONE you barely know? Obviously, I knew my mother because, as a single parent, she raised my sister and me. Meanwhile, my dad was a recurring character throughout my childhood. It was as if he was important enough to maintain a leading role in my life's sitcom, but often made the famous applause-inducing cameo appearances when he entered the scene like a beloved recurring guest star. His visits were brief yet impressionable. It was not until after he'd leave that his absence made me realize there was something missing.

"MAMA'S BABY, DADDY'S MAYBE"

My earliest memory of my dad was during a visit to our home when I was four. He was a tall, brown man with a round bald head. He had prominent eyebrows and a mustache to match. He was a cool cat who frequently wore a straw fedora hat and netted shirt with matching shoes. His shorts revealed the hairiest legs I had ever seen. His stride came straight out of the 1970s and no matter how many times he changed cars, he maintained a Cadillac Sedan Deville. His family background is somewhat complicated. He is the younger of the two children born between his mother and father. His mother was a foster parent to four children whom she later adopted, giving my father four additional siblings. Dad's youngest brother on his father's side was born outside his parents' relationship. I am unsure about the circumstances behind Dad's youngest brother's birth, but I could tell Dad did not like it.

Though I do not know much about the particulars of his upbringing, I learned he and my mother met during high school. Dad attended North Central and his mother was Mom'ela's guidance counselor at Arsenal Technical where I would later graduate in 2002. Dad told me that his mother was so fond of Mom'ela that she introduced them to each other. He graduated a semester early and served in the Navy for four years before returning to Indianapolis in 1982. Two years later, I was born. Mom'ela made sure I knew who my dad was when he visited during the earlier years.

Those visits were sporadic throughout elementary and nonexistent during the dark periods of junior high school, but Dad made attempts to connect with me once I got to high school. During my junior year, he offered me a used car that needed more repairs than feasible to drive it off his property. It was a car I would need to invest money in, but it was a car nonetheless. I passed on it because the TLC needed was more than I could afford. Yet, his attempt to gift his daughter with something significant was something I held dear to my heart. The following year, I invited him to my graduation ceremony. Apparently, he was in attendance but I would not have known except for the flowers he left with my mother to give to me. Upon hearing he slipped out early, I immediately felt hurt he did not stay. I couldn't remain sad for long, though, because that day was filled with so much joy. I was surrounded by family and friends who loved me unconditionally and nothing was going to keep me from celebrating the momentous occasion. I did what I always do and pushed the hurt under the rug.

DATING DADDY

Once I went off to college, my communication with Dad somewhat increased. We did not speak every day, but we did regular check-ins over the phone. It was not until I was twenty that I began to establish a deeper bond with him. On the eve of my senior year of college, Dad and I were having a conversation over the phone when he asked the question that had been the elephant in the room throughout our entire relationship.

> *"I cried uncontrollably for the little girl who wanted her father to embrace her."*

"Would you like to know why I was not a part of your life?" Immediately my heart stopped. My eyes welled with tears.

My grandmother had always had the proclivity for being "honest" while freely telling everyone's business or family rumors. She had shared with me many times before the "truth" about my dad. According to GMa, my dad was not an active parent because there was confusion about the identity of my real father. She said my mom believed I could either be the child of the man I came to know as my dad or another man she was dating throughout my parent's on-again off-again relationship.

Now I was about to hear Dad's side of the story for the first time. It was like waiting to hear the results of a paternity test on the Maury show, but it was my reality. Dad began by expressing how he wanted to be a part of my life and other things that I have since forgotten. Then he said it: Out of his own mouth, he confirmed what GMa had long suggested. He said Mom told him that he may not have been my father.

Upon hearing this, my heart dropped and my eyes couldn't hold back the tears anymore. I thought GMa was just speaking lies about my father's absence, but his words confirmed what she had said long ago. I cried uncontrollably for the little girl who wanted her father to embrace her. For the teenage girl who wanted her father's approval before going on her first date. For the young woman I had become without his protection or guidance. I couldn't stop the tears as he explained that he wanted us to grow closer from this moment forward, regardless of our past. I agreed and saw this moment as the beginning of the relationship I so craved to have with him.

"BROTHERS AIN'T IT"

We spoke throughout my senior year of college until an opportunity to deepen our relationship surfaced. My expected graduation date had been delayed by a semester, and since I had lived in the city for all four years, summers included, I was over the idea of spending another three months in the college town. My dad and his wife offered me a room for the summer in their home in my hometown, so I took it. Not only would this be a great opportunity to escape but to also build a better connection with him. What I did not anticipate was that I would be in summer school yet again, but it was not in a classroom. I would be schooled on the behaviors of men—by my own dad!

His lectures usually occurred at the most inconvenient times. Either I was rushing for work or preparing for a date. These teachable moments were inspired by whatever television show he was viewing at the time. Usually, the show would involve a man who did something clumsy and Dad would respond with, "See, that's the type of dumb stuff men do!" I'd pause and turn toward him as he continued, saying "we" make ridiculous mistakes and cause things to happen to "us." Even if Dad had turned on the television in the middle of the scene, he was certain the man was guilty without knowing the backstory of the show or commercial. He was convinced that all men have made, always make, and will continue to make thoughtless choices and are deserving of whatever consequences they face.

Other times, Dad's instructions were based on his random thoughts. He'd say (and I'm censoring), "Brothers ain't it" on a whim! If "that's the type of dumb stuff men do" was used to teach me about the silly things men did, "brothers ain't it" was a more serious assertion, teaching me about the things men did that hurt the women they claim they love. For instance, if a man broke his lady's heart through infidelity or lying, Dad would go into a "brothers ain't it" rant. The irony in all of this is that he may have exhibited some of the same behaviors he now disapproved of. Even still, I developed respect for him as I could see a moral standard underpinning his words, and I felt that this summer served as redemption for the relationship we did not cultivate earlier.

Most of the time his "brothers ain't it" talks occurred on days I had a date planned. You'd have expected me to cancel my plans for the evening and for the rest of my life after hearing him put down every man on the planet like that. I did not. To his credit, my dad helped me see guys' intentions more clearly and I was better able to filter some of the mischievous men who approached me throughout that summer. But it did not keep me from dating.

What's more, my dad reaffirmed me regularly. Every day he told me how I was a beautiful young lady and that I could have any man I wanted. Dad would then detail all the qualities that made me appealing and a great catch. He seemed to think highly of me, although he knew little about me—and I believed him.

Aside from the lessons shared and affirmations I received, Dad's lifestyle proved to be as instructive as his words. He made me reconsider some of the stereotypes I believed about masculinity. One belief I held was that women were the primary chefs of the home, but Dad knew how to cook. He even got me to like runny eggs, which I absolutely hated until that summer. Another belief I held was that men did not do chores around the home. However, my dad was the ultimate handyman and would make the home smell Lysol clean after he mopped the wooden floors throughout.

Gradually, my dad's words that summer began to change the way I perceived men. I started to consider his judgments and statements more seriously because he was a man himself. As an authority on masculinity, he had to know that behind every chivalrous smile was a man who could have bad intentions, who could be foul, disrespectful, and manipulative if you did not maintain boundaries. One guy I dated that summer, Leo, would later confirm the warnings my dad tried to convey to me.

FROM RELIGIOUS TO SPIRITUAL

The summer of 2006 was epic to say the least! Not only did it mark the beginning of my relationship with my dad, but I experienced a shift in my spiritual walk. No longer was I going to church only to escape life at home, but also to grow and seek a spiritual relationship with God. I had a strong desire to pursue God in a new way and began to question old beliefs I had become accustomed to.

In particular, I began contemplating God's omnipresence. If He is everywhere all the time, why wouldn't He be with me at home? Why did I need to attend church to experience His presence? In no way was I intending to never step foot in a church again, but I had reached the point where I questioned why I was going to church. *Why was Shavonne choosing to go to church?* This question involved an objective evaluation of my heart and check-up on my intentions.

In my heart, I was solid in my acceptance of God and biblical principles. At the core of my being, I believed in God and knew

He positioned me wherever I was at any given point in life for a specific purpose. I still acknowledged the relevancy of God's Word for everyday living. But God began dealing within me not only as it relates to my motives for attending church but also in my reasons for giving tithes and offerings. In Hebrews, the Bible says that the word of God is living and active and that it judges the thoughts and intentions of the heart—and I saw this work of God welling up inside me.

Anyone who regularly attends church may have heard at least one sermon or a series of messages on the topic of giving. And I fully receive the principles of stewardship as outlined in the Bible. But what I came to realize was that I had gotten to a place in my walk with God where I was trying to do all the right things to win Him over rather than from an overflow of love.

Take heed that you do not do your charitable deeds before men, to be seen by them. Otherwise you have no reward from your Father in heaven.
~Matthew 6:1

It was not as if I wanted to be seen by others, but I wanted to be seen by God. And I did so in the way a child wants to be "caught" doing a good deed by her parent. In college, I led the ministries I was involved in with a humble heart. But as time passed, I became more competitive with having the "best" ministry in the church and in the local community, all because I was passionate about my ministry work. After a while, my focus had shifted from ministering to performing. No longer was I trying to win people for God, but my choreography for the praise dances became more about entertaining the people who filled the pews.

Likewise, I had approached giving in a religious way rather than from my heart. I gave ten percent of my gross income out of obligation or church guilt. But God began to work on me in this area before I moved in with my dad the summer of 2006. He built upon my core belief that I was to bless others and share generously with His gifts to me and I was fortunate He blessed me with summer employment at a time when it seemed I could not secure a job. When I received my paychecks, I began praying and sought God's guidance as to where I should sow the financial seed.

I was now giving freely to whatever causes seemed worthwhile to me and where I could see immediate impact. Mom'ela said I used to throw cash out the window of the moving car as a toddler and this must have been what it felt like. I shared with others because I felt I had more than enough from God. It was as if He positioned me in front of people and causes He wanted me to distribute His wealth to. It all belongs to Him in the first place, but I was beyond happy and willing to do it. I finally felt I was moving beyond the religious act of going to church and giving to becoming a woman motivated by God's spirit within me.

In the process, my heart was transformed. Giving went from an act of duty to one of pure joy! It was both emancipating and exhilarating to give from a grateful heart. This was the first time in my adulthood that I gave from my heart like the cheerful giver in 2 Corinthians 9:7.

CRUCIAL CROSSROADS

As the summer was coming to a close, Dad and I agreed to keep in contact. We made meaningful strides in our relationship and I grew to respect him more than I had ever before. I planned to include him in more life events as they came up. Who knew? Maybe any future boyfriends would be pre-screened by Dad before they could seriously date me. It would have been nice to witness Dad sizing the guy up, talking with him man to man, and warning him against taking advantage of his daughter. As I packed up my car to return to campus for my last semester, my hope was that the summer of 2006 would be the beginning of a lifelong relationship with my father.

I found Mom'ela's maxim, "Nothing changes if nothing changes," to be true for life as well as relationships. My relationship with my dad did not change much after I moved out because we did not make an intentional effort to change it. Instead of growing closer, our relationship returned to what it had been before. Distant.

I invited him to my graduation from undergrad that December and he did not show. Given his previous track record, it wasn't as if I expected him to be there. I did, however, think he would have made more of an effort since we had grown closer just a few months before.

Our communication remained spotty even after I returned to Indianapolis in January 2007. I moved in with a friend from college, Christyn, and her family with a vow to move out before her wedding five months later. I appreciated her parents for the love they demonstrated by taking in a girl they barely knew as their third child. To avoid overextending my welcome, I stayed occupied and spent more nights away than in the home. Christyn's father recognized my absence and lovingly called me the "prodigal daughter." What is even more interesting is when Christyn's father inquired about my family background and realized he grew up with my dad.

Years had passed and my dad and I had only spoke in November when I'd called to wish him happy birthday. Dad's eldest son Rick was the constant link to my father's side of the family. Though we are eight years apart, my eldest brother pursued a relationship with me with the effort I had hoped my dad would show. He sought me out on multiple occasions to establish a sibling bond and to keep me updated on Dad.

Because our relationship had turned distant again, I no longer felt the need for Dad's validation when I began a long-term relationship with Deion in 2010. I knew the relationship was unique and we began officially dating on our own terms. When he proposed two years later, the question arose as to who would walk me down the aisle. I asked my mother's father, GPa, to do so because he was a consistent role model throughout my life. It gave him great joy and it was an experience I would not have changed for the world.

Two or three days before the wedding, I received an unexpected call from Dad. It had been at least a year or two since the last time we spoke, but he had gotten my number from Mom'ela. His voice was warm and he sounded genuinely happy for his eldest daughter to be tying the knot. He asked details about the ceremony and expressed how he wanted to attend if I would have him. I told him yes even though inside I was already hopeless and trying to protect my heart from the inevitable—but the daughter deep down wanted her daddy to be there.

Do you know who did not show up to the wedding? You guessed it!

Upon returning from our honeymoon, I called Dad to ask why he was not in attendance. He told me he had picked up a job at the last minute and he regretted not being there. This time, his excuse did not work for me. I couldn't continue acting as if his absence did not matter and he needed to be responsible for following through with his promises. In a respectful manner, I told him I would have appreciated a phone call to say he couldn't make it. Surprisingly, he was receptive to my comment and said he would make more of an effort to communicate with me in the future.

DATING DADDY

After that conversation, my dad and I rarely talked until I informed him of my divorce almost two years later.

At the beginning of this chapter I posed the question, How do you honor someone you barely know? To this day, I still do not know. And I'm still in the process of learning how to do this. Though my dad was not involved in most of my life, I choose to believe he did what he could, considering the circumstances of my birth. There are many opportunities I felt I missed out on and lessons I did not receive growing up. And I believe I have forgiven him for most of it, but there are some issues that linger to this day.

CHAPTER 5

SILVER LINING

When things go wrong, don't go with them.
~Elvis Presley

STUDIES SHOW THAT THE LACK of a father's involvement negatively impacts a daughter's well-being. Fatherless daughters typically act out in school, become depressed, and abuse drugs. But I was fortunate to have positive role models to keep me on track. Where some people viewed the challenges my sister and I faced as negative, I saw them as opportunities to beat the odds. Those obstacles could not dictate the type of woman I would become. The generational curses and traditional behaviors that have long plagued my family would not have to be my reality. I refused to become a product of my environment or a negative statistic as indicated in the research regarding women with similar upbringings as me.

TWO PARENTS OR NOT TWO PARENTS?

Contrary to popular belief, not all children from two-parent homes fare better than those raised in single-parent households. There are instances where it is more beneficial to a child's well-being when the father lives elsewhere. In a study by social demographers Alan Booth, Mindy Scott, and Valarie King, the emotional closeness between adolescents and their fathers was used to determine its effects on their self-esteem, delinquency, performance in school, depression, and substance abuse. From the onset of their study, they believed the attribute of closeness is "protective and beneficial to children and can be cultivated regardless of residential status" of the biological father.

In the study, the researchers compared the differences between adolescents with residential fathers to those whose fathers did not live in the home. Ultimately, the most beneficial environment for a child is to have a father in the home who is emotionally connected with them. Among their other findings, however, was that it is better to have a close relationship with a nonresidential father rather than a distant relationship with a residential one. In other words, some fathers may have a more meaningful relationship with their children even if they do not live in the same home as the child.

> *"Why isn't more emphasis placed on the quality of the relationship a daughter has with her father?"*

But if the quality of the relationship is most important, why does our culture primarily measure a parent's involvement by the amount of money given in child support? There are obvious costs to raising a child and they are not inexpensive by any means. But why isn't more emphasis placed on the quality of the relationship a daughter has with her father? What if the real reason he is unable to give his princess the world is because he spends much of his time working a minimum wage job? What if the father is insecure about himself and his inability to contribute, thus causing him to retreat in shame?

Scholars Wrenetha Julion, Deborah Gross, Gina Barclay-McLaughlin, and Louis Fogg understood this and sought to get the other side of the story—from the fathers. In particular, they solicited the perspective of nonresidential African-America fathers on their contributions and perceptions of their involvement in their children's lives. In the study, all the fathers in the focus groups shared the sentiment that their "involvement was impeded by their own insecurities, imperfections, and conflicts as well as the doubts, fears, and concerns of others." These men did not feel equipped for the task of being a good father to their children. Some did not have their father's involvement to model after while others did not have adequate resources. In particular, they did not have workshops or a support system that could teach them how to be a good father while living in a separate home. This made me wonder how my dad perceived his involvement in my life and his parenting skills. Did he have similar insecurities about his ability to raise me?

Whether my dad had insecurities or felt inadequate, I never realistically expected him to be with my mother. This could be because I became accustomed from an early age to live without him in the home. Maybe the love I received from our village filled most my tank. Yet, I only realized something was missing or felt the holes in my heart following his brief visits.

This void is a shared emotion among women whose fathers have moved on after their relationship with the mothers ended. Clinical Social Worker Janice Marie Houston-Little, Ph.D., weaved the narratives of the women she interviewed for her dissertation as it relates to their experiences with their fathers. She, as well as the women she interviewed, wished their fathers knew they still needed them even after things did not work out with their mothers.

Similarly, I wonder if my dad understood that I wanted a relationship with him even when I couldn't communicate it. I did not expect him and Mom'ela to maintain a relationship, yet I hoped there was some way he could have maintained a relationship with me. By the time I had the language to express this, my dad was unavailable. What's more, I didn't feel we had the type of relationship where I had the right to express this need. Would he even be receptive to a conversation of this nature?

A SIBLING RIVALRY OF SORTS

I am the third oldest of his four children. My eldest brother, Rick, is eight years older than me and is the one I speak with the most. I am unsure the age difference between my second eldest brother and I, but my youngest sibling is sixteen years my junior. Of the four of us, it appears Dad has a closer relationship with the boys than my sister and I.

Would he be open to explaining why it appears he has a stronger bond with his other children and a mere association with me? Yes, we had our groundbreaking conversation during college that provided some clarity about this, but I still longed to understand this on a deeper level. Did he still have hang-ups regarding his paternity? Even if we took a paternity test today, what difference would it make? Years have gone by and I have accumulated more memories with guys I've dated short-term than with the man who is listed on my birth certificate.

Apparently, my perception of Dad's attentiveness to my older brothers was not anything out of the ordinary. Journalist Victoria Secunda also noted that "noncustodial fathers try harder to stay in touch with sons than with daughters." Throughout his house, there are pictures of my brothers and their families as well as pictures of my dad with my brothers during their childhood. There were even pictures of my little sister, but none of me. I am hurt every time I visit his home and see the pictures on display. What was so different about his relationship with his youngest daughter than with me? Why hadn't he worked to have a relationship with me?

Or was it that once he tried to connect with me, I pushed him away? Did I create an impenetrable wall in the name of being strong "with or without" this man like the women in my family instructed me to do? For the most part, I am thankful for the woman they have helped me to become, but I now realize I may have played a role in the distance between my dad and me.

For instance, when I was sixteen he offered me a car. One would think I would be appreciative of this, but I was not. The car was an older model convertible. I would have been one of the few students at my high school who had a convertible, but the driver's side door didn't open properly. Neither did the door to the gas tank. The car needed so much work it was not worth driving off his front lawn!

But this was my dad's first attempt at giving me something worthwhile. I should have been more grateful, but instead what I wanted most was what I perceived he gave my siblings: quality time. If you asked Dad about his children today, he would be able to give a status report on my brothers and sister.

"This son lives here and is working as a _____."

"My other son's children are doing this or that."

"My youngest daughter is participating in this or that organization in school."

"Shavonne is???"

But there were things I didn't know about him as well. I called Dad to learn more about his background to include in this book. He just so happened to return my call as I was preparing to watch the season-six finale of *The Walking Dead*! I looked at my phone and I looked at the TV. I looked at the TV and looked down at the phone, contemplating whether we should talk at this very moment. It was the season finale, after all, where they would be introducing the worst antagonist in the TWD series, NEGAN! I thought...

Did I want to meet Negan with the rest of the loyal TWD fans in real time?

DATING DADDY

Or should I value "people over things" like Suze Orman tells her followers?

This was a real conundrum for me... Nonetheless, I sacrificed watching the season finale live to speak with my dad.

During this conversation I learned how he and my mother met. I learned more about the regrets in his career and how he had not taken advantage of certain opportunities he wished he had. He caught me up on the ten years between the epic summer of 2006 and this moment. When he asked my age, I felt myself becoming upset and thought sarcastically, *Shouldn't you know the age difference between my eldest brother and me?*

Or better yet, my little sister and me???

I exhaled and reminded myself that he did return my call and the conversation was good until this point. As we prepared to hang up, he welcomed me to visit him more frequently and to bring some pictures of me by the house. As of this writing, I have not followed through with his invitation.

DEFYING THE ODDS

Nothing, however, will take the place of our summer together. In my mind, there was no experience passed or yet to come that will ever compare to the three months I spent in my father's home. It answered many questions and unveiled the man behind the myth. To witness his lifestyle, the way he did work around the house or was totally engaged in the game on TV, all seemed spectacular after going what seemed like forever without it. Over the years, I have maintained platonic relationships with men who gave me insight into the male perspective. But nothing came close to my dad's words of wisdom. His "Brothers ain't it" rants and explanations of "dumb stuff men do" accompanied by his unique mannerisms are forever a part of my memory. Many of my longings were filled once I lived with my dad the summer of 2006.

But what about the potential damage from the years leading to that life changing summer? There are plenty of studies that describe the negative effects caused by the lack of a connection with one's biological father, but I am fortunate to be an exception. Where my grades could have suffered from the instability in our home, I excelled in my courses. In fact, it wasn't until I began submitting applications to colleges my senior year of high school that I learned I was graduating fourth out of 250 students in my class. I held a strong belief in my academic abilities, even in the face of the insecurities I often felt throughout my life.

I was not violent nor did I use drugs, but I have battled depression at various points throughout my life. The first time I remember being depressed was in seventh grade when my sister and I were put into foster care. After my failed suicide attempt, I was sad for what felt like a long time. On the outside, I probably appeared extremely happy (I blame it on the Prozac). But on the inside, I felt lost, unsure of what the future held and unmotivated to make new friends.

In high school, however, something shifted for me. I began to envision the independence I would have as an adult. I dreamed new dreams. I aspired to become an obstetrician/gynecologist, but I only wanted "to deliver babies, not the other part." My teachers did all they could to prepare me for post-secondary education. School, like the church, was my sanctuary. My safe place. My teachers affirmed me, challenged me, and gave me the outlet I needed.

With each pat on the back or nod of approval, my need to succeed went into overdrive. In fact, it became a rat race to me. I had to prove I could succeed without my dad and in spite of my circumstances. I had something to prove to myself and to anyone who was not a part of my life. I had to prove I was worthwhile and that they were missing out on this wonderful human being. This beautiful, talented, and intelligent young lady was worth getting to know more deeply. I would show them!

Long before I learned to love my supporters, I was on a mission to prove the naysayers wrong. The naysayers were not necessarily the people who said negative things; they were the people who didn't say anything at all, including my dad. He wasn't my sole motivation for my academic success, but he was in the silent audience of people I had to prove something to. I pushed myself and fought to defy the odds to the point of building an impenetrable emotional wall. I had no time to invest in my feelings because I had things to accomplish. I put so much energy into proving I did not need him that I went to college guarded, even minimizing my own accomplishment of making it here.

Behold, I will do a new thing, now it shall spring forth; shall you not know it? I will even make a road in the wilderness and rivers in the desert.
~Isaiah 43:19

NO SUCH THING AS A DEAD END

When I think of all the research and statistics on the fate of children without a residential father, I am reminded that God can make a way where there seems to be no way. I believe God blessed me with a plethora of uncles whose love filled me when I felt deserted by my dad.

My maternal uncles were amazing! GMa's mother was a Blackfoot Indian and her father was of Irish decent. As a result, my five-foot-tall grandmother had fair skin. And many of her children had different fathers. It always fascinated me to see the various hues of my aunts and uncles and, as a kid, I associated them with celebrities. One of my eldest uncles reminded me of actor Denzel Washington, but he passed away before I really got to know him. The fourth eldest son looked like singer-songwriter El DeBarge with swag. The fifth son reminded me of rapper Heavy D in stature and personality because he was the life of the party. But I was closest to GMa's youngest son, and the baby of the bunch, who was a mix between actor Tom Cruise's look, nose included, with the personality of rapper TuPac. His father was Sicilian and this uncle was closest to the ages of my cousins and me. We shared a dream of becoming professional models and his passing took our family by storm because he was loved by all.

GMa had three daughters including my mother, but the only celebrity association I can remember making was between my aunt, who favors singer Gloria Estefan, and her husband who reminds me of singer-songwriter Phil Collins. As you probably inferred, they are an interracial couple. To me, they were the epitome of a Christian marriage. They attended church together, hosted Thanksgiving dinners, and were successful in their own right. My aunt loves to landscape and her projects make their home look straight out of the pages of *Home and Gardens.*

Uncle Phil Collins was a natural fit to our family—but not in the way some people try to assimilate to another culture when they are the minority. Uncle Phil Collins fit in because he never tried to be anything but himself, and that included a good sense of humor and care for others. I respected that he obviously cared for my aunt. He opened every door and ensured she had everything she needed. He shielded her from the world. Like my sister and I, my mom and her siblings endured many of the same hardships, but there were nine of them! Uncle Phil Collins helped Aunt Gloria heal from some of the trauma she experienced and protected her from any new hurt caused by anyone in our family.

DATING DADDY

Not only did Uncle Phil Collins care for my aunt, but he cared for my sister and I like we were his biological nieces. Since the day I met him at my cousin's birthday party long ago, he was a constant support and regularly checked on my sister and me. Throughout our upbringing, he and Aunt Gloria opened their home to us when things were shaky. If ever he or Aunt Gloria saw we had a need, without a question, they would bring it to us. When I took guardianship of my sister, for instance, they bought me a new bed and gave us furniture to fill the apartment. They also gave me a regular stipend every month from the day they dropped me off at college through my graduation four and a half years later.

Aside from his financial contributions, what I value most was Uncle Phil Collin's support after my husband left. He was the first relative to know, at least a month or two, before I informed the rest of our family. Out of all my biological uncles and family members, I opened up to an in-law because I knew I could trust him with sensitive news such as this. He continued to pray for my husband and me and to regularly check in on his niece when I was at my lowest state, and for that, I am more than grateful. When I felt like I could not see a way out of my wilderness, God blessed me with hope and encouragement through Uncle Phil Collins and He will do the same for you.

I want to leave you with this: When it appears that you are always at a disadvantage and never able to get ahead, trust that God can make a way out of no way. Society promotes two-parent households as if that's the only way you can be happy. You may feel ashamed because you were raised by your single grandmother. Don't be! Even if the odds seem stacked against you because of the imperfect circumstances of your upbringing, do not count yourself out. You can create a successful life that defies statistics and society's standards. Do not let society or research dictate your level of success or make you feel there's no other way in life. It may appear you'll never get a step ahead, but just know that God can bless you with water in the deserts of life—even when it appears to be an absolute drought.

CHAPTER 6

INSIGHT FROM DAD'S KNEE

IT HAS ALWAYS BEEN EASIER to acknowledge the men who made a positive impact in my life than to revere my biological father. They made me feel I could do no wrong in their sight and I grew up believing them. So, imagine the sobering reality check when I had to face my shortcomings! Regardless of a father's involvement, or lack thereof, we are responsible for how we treat and respond to him. Once I realized this, I went from standing at odds with my dad to the closeness of a daughter on her father's knee. The process of unlearning this skewed view of myself began once I faced my imperfections and further examined my relationship with the first man who gave me his last name.

DAUGHTER IN THE MIRROR

Now, raise your hand if you have ever pointed the finger at someone else when something went wrong in your life. Raise your hand if you justified something you did out of spite because someone hurt you. Raise your hand if you ever said something knowing your words would harm another. You can put your hands down now. You're probably in a very public place reading this and I don't want to embarrass you much further.

But the real question I have for you is, have you considered that there is one common person in all three of the above statements? Yes—it's *you*. You are responsible for the thoughts, words, and actions you put out there in the world. It is so much easier to blame others for our response to a situation. It's easier to justify how we treat another person whom we feel has wronged us without considering the part we played in the relationship.

The lack of connection between my dad and I was not as one-sided as I had believed for so long. It wasn't that he totally hated me and didn't care; I learned that he actually *did* care. And it wasn't just the issues between him and my mom that kept us apart. There was another person who played a role in the climate of our relationship, and that person was me. For the longest time, I internalized my dad's absence in a negative way and never challenged how my perception of him affected how I treated him. In the process of writing the previous chapter, I realized how my perception of him affected how I mistreated him the few times we interacted. Who knew the process of writing a memoir would lead to such introspection?

It all commenced with one burning question about a specific aspect of the father-daughter relationship. From there, I had sought out an article to answer that question and after reading the first article, another question surfaced. Then I began exploring various aspects of the father-daughter relationship, love, or other related topics. With every article, peer-reviewed journal, sermon, and book, I found myself learning about personal issues I may have realized before but could not articulate.

In the process, I became more appreciative of Mom'ela's struggles to raise us. To my surprise, I grew more compassionate toward my father. Most important, I realized I was not perfect. Here I was thinking I would find research to support my idea that absent fathers are the ones to blame for daughters who misbehaved—behaved badly in love, badly in life, and enjoyed self-destructive behaviors—when in fact, what I found out was we have a choice. *I* have a choice. We have responsibility for the direction of our own lives.

Yes, my dad lacked consistency, but when he tried to be a part of my life, what did I do? I pushed him away. I did not give him the opportunity to make a meaningful connection. Even after the epic summer of 2006, I left his home with the half-hope that the dynamics of our relationship would improve while half-doubting things would seriously change. Thus, I did not hold up my end of the bargain to communicate with him or visit regularly.

As you read this, you may be coming up with more reasons to see this differently. You may see the scales leaning more on his role than mine because, after all, he was "adulting" longer than me. After all, he knew what he was leaving behind when he and my mom ended their relationship. But at some point, I came to realize I had the power to change my life, and so do you. We have the power to try a new thing, to change our perspective on how we see the world. And when we change the way we see things, our lives shift gears.

So, while I was pointing the finger at my father, I was putting more focus on him than on the person I could control: me. While I was placing the blame on Dad, I strapped on my straitjacket of "victim" and gave him the power to affect my mood. I drove myself crazy trying to prove myself worthy of his affection. I even drove myself insane while mentally repeating unloving words that he "probably" thought about the daughter he left behind. He may have never thought ill of me, but I believed he did.

USE CIRCUMSTANCES AS MOTIVATION, NOT EXCUSES

Another lesson I learned from Dad was to use my circumstances to motivate me instead of using them as a crutch. In my heart, I believed I could change the direction of my life by the choices I made every day. I trusted God to position me in places I have never seen and I dreamed big! From a young age, I knew I wanted to explore the world. But I also knew I couldn't afford it. Fortunately, many opportunities to travel opened themselves to me. One experience I will never forget was going to Salvador da Bahia, Brazil, for a two-week study abroad course. It was both liberating and educational as I learned about the African experience in Brazil. I had not realized the influence and rich history of Africans in Latin America and it was an amazing experience to be immersed in the culture. Without a doubt, this remarkable opportunity stemmed from my choice to dream outside the limitations of my circumstances.

> "Every obstacle, limitation, or perceived disadvantage you face can appear to be working against you when in fact God promises He can and will use those very things to develop you—for your good."

As we have previously discussed in chapter five, the bulk of research and popular belief in society is that children of absent fathers suffer emotionally and are outperformed in the classroom by kids of two-parent homes. And to that I say, "But God!" God can turn what appears to be a dead or unsuitable soil and fertilize it for a beautiful, strong, and vibrant tree. You are a tree planted by God. Every obstacle, limitation, or perceived disadvantage you face can appear to be working against you when in fact God promises He can and will use those very things to develop you—for your good. Witnessing your parents face unemployment, for example, may show you how to prepare for the future once you begin working. Or, not having access to government assistance may motivate you to pursue that degree that leads to a lucrative career. And, because your parents established firm rules for dating, you may have avoided becoming a parent before you were prepared to do so.

If I had held on to any resentments regarding my father, I could have become a different woman than I am. Today, I am blessed to do work that brings me joy and to have experienced some of the adventures my career affords me. But I can only imagine the negative choices I could have made, and the excuse would have been "because Daddy wasn't there." I could have become a bully and antagonized people who had two parents at home. I could have become sexually active at an earlier age, but I was too afraid of becoming pregnant. I was frightened by the thought of raising a child when our lives were already unstable under Mom's care. I could have done so many things in the name of a truant father. Instead, I allowed his absence to motivate me.

This does not mean I wasn't sad or longed for a relationship with my dad. In fact, I did suffer from low self-esteem. For a long time, I thought other kids were better off than me. On the surface, they appeared to be living the life of relative luxury because they had the latest clothes and could afford to eat at restaurants regularly. However, I have come to learn that some parents buy their children's affection or use their ability to invest in materialism to bury their own insecurities. Sometimes parents use money to make up for quality time they're missing with their children. Meanwhile, other parents are motivated by what they didn't have when they were growing up. Behind their closed doors were closets of insecurities, beds of heartbreak, and complicated issues that made me appreciate what little I had.

Whether good or bad, our circumstances can sink or propel us to new heights. But, ultimately, we have the power to determine this. We have the power to proclaim "I WILL not look like what I have gone through!" And I am not saying to ignore your situation because doing so will lead to another set of problems. However, you can determine not to quit. You can make up your mind that you will not let the absence of a parent, father or mother, keep you from being great. You will defeat the odds and learn to treat others with respect, surround myself with people who nurture your spirit—and deal with your insecurities head-on instead of putting on a mask of lies.

HONORING FATHER...REVISITED

With that in mind, I'd like to reconsider the conundrum from chapter four. How do we keep God's commandment to honor someone whom we cannot see regularly? How do we regard our parents highly if we have lost respect for them? As I wrote chapter four, I could not see how this would be possible. It may have been possible for others, but certainly not for me. Since then, I have had a conversation with my "brother from another mother," Daniel, and he shone light on this dilemma. We shared a common history of absentee fathers and mothers who were addicted to chemical substances. Both of us share common spiritual beliefs and possess a strong desire to change trends and traditions that have been passed down from generation to generation. We want to change our family trees.

In so many words, Daniel stated we must see the best in our parents. That is how we honor them. He said we must treat them with the same regard we do for kings and queens.

Considering Daniel's explanation, I tried to visualize treating my dad with the same level of respect as a king. Since America does not operate under a monarchy system, I would have to show respect like I would for the president, local government officials, or my supervisor. A supervisor! I could conceptualize this!

I found it easier to understand treating my father like a supervisor than trying to define "honoring" him. The problem is that my supervisor, in this case, is much like Charlie from the

DATING DADDY

TV show *Charlie's Angels*. I don't see him nor do we communicate frequently. He checks in with the same swiftness as he checks out.

When I was bitter about this, I would refer to my dad by his full government name. Even worse, I would mention him as "the man on my birth certificate." That was a low blow, I know, but it was obvious I didn't honor or respect him. It seriously took that summer at his home to change my perspective and begin to see him as a human who has flaws instead of a malicious person at heart. Any distance between us since 2006 was not due to enmity; it was because we had become so accustomed to how infrequently we saw each other and failed to maintain the relationship that formed.

My hope is that you'll begin to reconsider the way you view the people in your life. You must be determined to honor or think highly of the people who are not easy to love. You must be intentional in treating them with the utmost respect, as much as you can. It will sound so cliché, but life is too short not to. Having lost relatives, friends, and role models earlier than expected, I have gained an appreciation for celebrating every day that God has blessed me with. Though my dad and I do not talk every day, I am more willing to initiate a meaningful call here and there than I had before. I don't want to live with the regret that I never tried to bridge the gap between us because I held on to old hurts and issues. I refuse to carry that baggage anymore.

I still have unanswered questions I'd like to ask my dad when the time is right. Whether I get the answers to them or not, I want to take our relationship beyond the superficial level it has operated on for so long. I've learned it's not healthy to dismiss people without ever really giving them an opportunity. Our fathers deserve a chance to mend the broken relationships with us, but sometimes we must be the adult and initiate this process.

Sometimes a father does not understand what's missing until the concerns are brought to him.

This process of reflecting on the relationship between my father and I has healed me in ways I would have never imagined. It revealed the holes I hadn't recognized before, including behaviors I carried into my other relationships. Particularly, my motivation to succeed and experiences of deep sadness stemmed from the issues in our relationship. Now that you have met the man whom I call Dad, I will use our relationship to shine light on the romantic relationships that followed that epic summer of 2006. But before we do, we'll look back at the first man to steal my heart, the one who laid the groundwork for me to even be open to my father: my college sweetheart, Cliff.

CLIFF:
Dating for Daddy Heartbreak

Shavonne's involvement with the Black Cultural Center afforded her a once in a lifetime opportunity to meet and dance for Dr. Maya Angelou. Pictured here with "Christyn" in February 2003.

CHAPTER 7

LOVE ESCAPADE

BY THE TIME I GRADUATED from high school in 2002, I had experienced so much distress that I became overprotective with my heart. It was nearly impossible for anyone new to know me beyond the surface, and my ambition was in overdrive. I knew going to college was important and I viewed it as a checkmark on my life's to-do list. Unfortunately, that is not the way life was meant to be. Life is more than doing. It is a process of becoming that allows you to experience both sides of a position. Sometimes you are the greatest victim and, if you live long enough, you will become the greatest culprit. I thought remaining closed and guarded would be the best way for me to move through life. I did not think I would ever experience anything other than that. In fact, I underestimated the value of being open until I met my college sweetheart, Cliff. Our journey liberated me and soothed my heart before I moved in with my dad the summer of 2006.

ONE FOOT IN, ONE FOOT OUT

During the first year of undergrad, I attended various places of worship near campus until someone introduced me to a local Baptist church known as the "Miracle on 18th Street." The interim pastor connected with college-aged students like me and filled the pews with young adults each Sunday. Meanwhile, I was beginning the process of obtaining guardianship of my sister, who was now sixteen years old, and I knew I needed God and the help of others to do this, so I joined the church at the beginning of my sophomore year.

My involvement in ministry commenced soon after the interim pastor was voted as the official shepherd of the church. He maintained a vision for using the members' natural talents and abilities for the work of God and the church. When Pastor learned I was majoring in theatre, he charged me to develop and lead a drama ministry at the church. This was the furthest thing from my mind! Don't get me wrong—I love the performing arts, but I didn't love it enough to be involved with it both on campus and outside of class time. Nonetheless, I accepted the assignment and began preparing for the upcoming Christmas musical using the skills I had learned from my studies at school.

It turned out to be a great musical for the holidays and I received praise from fellow members and visitors, but soon my focus shifted toward a new ministry I was more passionate about. When Pastor announced a call-out for the new praise dance ministry, I contacted the leader as soon as church was dismissed. With the growth spurt in our church membership, new ministries were being developed regularly and this was one I could not pass up! The leader was an upperclassman at the university I attended and was in the sorority I was interested in joining, so this opportunity to connect was a win-win situation.

Together, we choreographed several dances before I succeeded her and expanded the ministry's reputation beyond the four walls of the church. What started off as a small group for anyone with even limited dance experience who wanted to participate, grew to one group for youth and another for adults. The youth dance ministry could minister on any given Sunday without my guidance. Meanwhile Divine Praise, the adult dance group, ministered both at church and on campus for various events. After watching the movie *What's Love Got to Do with*

It for the millionth time, I was inspired to create an annual "Praise Dance Revue," which was a ministry spinoff of the Ike Turner Revue. This annual service was hosted by our church and included dance ministries from all over the state who would share the gospel through dance.

As I grew in my faith and commitment to Christ in the ministry, I felt conflicted about my lifestyle outside the church. I'd attend the services throughout the week and lead rehearsals for the ministry. Fridays and Saturdays, though, were spent at the local college parties, which sometimes led to my exhaustion during Sunday's service. After a while I wondered how I was supposed to lead a ministry while enjoying secular thrills.

> *Keep your heart with all diligence,*
> *for out of it spring the issues of life.*
> *~Proverbs 4:23*

Something had to give. Either I was going to follow the more worldly desires of my heart and risk my imperfections being revealed in my ministry work, or I would submit my lifestyle to Christ as much as I humanly could and produce good fruit. Looking back, I know this was a critical decision in my faith walk.

Ultimately, I decided to focus on Christ and the ministry, a choice that proved to be worth the sacrifice. And things blossomed once I turned and made that commitment. To stay relevant, I asked the teenagers to teach me the contemporary dances and I found ways to incorporate some of them into the choreography for Divine Praise. I also included some of the choreography of my favorite artist of all time: Michael Jackson! This alone helped the youth stay committed to the ministry when they could have been persuaded by their peers to leave. To be able to make God relevant to them fulfilled me in an indescribable way and I loved it! It still amazes me that God used my mess, my inconsistencies, and my budding spiritual maturity to bless a multitude of people both inside and outside of the "Miracle on 18th Street."

COMEDY & TRAGEDY

Ministry was not the only thing that brought fulfillment during undergrad. I also enjoyed the company of an upperclassman. I don't remember exactly how I met Cliff sometime near the beginning of my freshman year, but when you're one of the few African Americans in a theatre program, you kind of stick out like a sore thumb. I was a performing arts student while his area of focus was production. We became instant friends, and that friendship blossomed to something more.

For as long as I can remember, I've wanted to be with a man who "can switch from a suit to sweats seamlessly." In other words, I like a man who is a professional and could accompany me at black-tie affairs, but with the same ease can assume a more playful nature as the sweat pants imply. One who can fill a room with laughter and who I can enjoy life with in our relaxed private moments.

Cliff was a man in sweats. He was a very playful man with serious eyes and the cutest nose.

While seeking guardianship of my sister, Cliff supported me throughout the process. He would take my sister and me grocery shopping as needed. Cliff also found ways to help me enjoy being a young woman by taking me to the movies and on car rides throughout the city. I didn't think much of it because I was still naïve to the dating scene and the advances of "real" men. Looking back, however, I should have realized he was interested in me because he drove more cautiously in the beginning as he was getting to know me. Later, he would drive like a speed demon after

DATING DADDY

we'd known each other for a while. We stayed in touch on and off for a few months, but when the busyness of school picked-up and my responsibilities of being a single guardian consumed me, we slowly lost touch as sophomore year rolled on.

Cliff and I reconnected sometime during my junior year. By this time, things were more stable for my sister and I and Cliff regularly visited our home. He and I chatted often and I found it easy to talk to him about anything. Before I met him, I built up walls to protect myself. After Cliff and I had been friends for a while, our conversations went beyond the surface. He could read my expressions and notice if I was hiding the truth about my feelings and would probe in the most compassionate way. Over time, I felt safe and became less defensive toward him and others.

Second semester of junior year, I had an epiphany that would take our relationship to the next level. I considered his consistency, care, and support during the time we had known each other and wondered how he felt about me. One evening, we were sitting in my kitchen when I asked him if he had ever thought about us dating officially. By the end of the conversation, we were exclusively together.

Our relationship became my refuge when I reached an educational crossroads that semester. After repeatedly being rejected for acting roles, I began to give up hope and stopped attending my theatre classes. Instead, I spent most of my time at his place watching reruns of *A Different World* and eating whatever meal he prepared for us.

When I did go to campus, I spent a lot of time with my mentor, Mr. William Caise. He was the assistant director of the Black Cultural Center where I had danced, worked, and spent considerable time studying. Mr. Caise had pursued a career on stage and understood the complexities of being a Black theatre major at a predominately White institution. He also knew about my family background and provided a great shoulder to cry on regarding academic and personal matters. Though I had taken a personal sabbatical from my studies, I was very present in Mr. Caise's office, my extracurricular activities, and at Cliff's apartment.

After missing approximately six weeks of classes, I met with my assigned faculty mentor in the theatre department to express my discouragement in what became an emotional conversation. My sentiment was well received by my mentor who stated that it was the type of vulnerability I needed to tap into for my roles. I was astonished! Was it really that simple? Soon after, I returned to class and worked diligently to make up the assignments and projects I had missed.

Upon my return, Cliff began to change as he had been doing some soul searching himself. He had given up on the theatre program that brought us together because he didn't see a future career in it. He contemplated his next moves and joined the National Guard and was scheduled to leave for basic training by the end of the spring semester.

I DO...

It was the summer of 2005. Cliff wrote me often from the military base and even made calls home when he could. After weeks apart, I could not wrap my mind around a long-distance relationship with a man in the military. It felt as if he was in jail because he was inaccessible to me. He described feelings of isolation from the outside world; every correspondence from him was filled with a longing for home, and my heart felt pity for him.

Imagine my surprise when after just two or three months, Cliff returned home unexpectedly due to a knee injury. This man who was once built like a tight end in the NFL now looked as small as an athlete in high school from the amount of weight he lost in basic training. Though he came back as a different man, one thing that remained was his spontaneity. That summer, I was in school and was having a rough day. I guess the stress was written all over my face when I saw Cliff and this prompted him to get me out of my head. When he said, "Let's go," I resisted. I had homework to do and a checklist of tasks to complete. I didn't have time for one of his adventures and I threw a temper tantrum. Like a real temper tantrum! Childish, I know.

When he finally got me to get in the car, I sunk in the passenger seat and turned my body away from him. I was not ready to give in any time soon. It was a long car ride and when it was time to get out of the car, I realized we had driven to the nearest amusement park. As we walked across the bridge from the admissions stand into the park, I felt the tension in my face start to relax. No matter how much I resisted, Cliff's adventure slowly wore my guards down. By the end of the night, the rides, weather, and romanticism of being swept away made it one of the best days of my life. Cliff had a way of making life less serious and getting me out of my head.

Another random adventure occurred later that summer after my twenty-first birthday. That evening, Cliff and I were relaxing at my place when he, again, wanted to take me on a spontaneous car drive. We talked about going to a park and decided to go to the one near the movie theatre off-campus. It was a beautiful evening. One of the first things I noticed as we got out of the car was the sky. It was as lit as a constellation exhibit in a planetarium. The park surrounded us in a deep blue night that was dark enough to calm one's spirit but visible enough to find our way toward the park bench. Once we sat down, I noticed the radiance of the trees filled with leaves that subtly waved to and fro. It sounds like a scene in a romantic movie, right?

There on that park bench we sat and talked comfortably, a conversation no different than any we'd had before. We discussed our goals and the future. He mentioned things he enjoyed about me and how much our relationship meant to him, which was nothing out of the ordinary for him to do. This time, though, he finished what he was saying by asking me to marry him! He said he has planned to officially propose soon, but the ambiance of the evening created the perfect setting for the proposal.

I said yes!

Because it was impromptu, he did not have a ring to make it official and said he planned to buy one soon. I didn't mind being without a ring because he had a track record of going above and beyond for me. This was the man who found a need and did whatever was necessary to fulfill it regularly. After all, I knew I loved Cliff and that he cared enough for me to protect my heart for a lifetime.

Days later, we began shopping for rings. Because I had another year of school, we knew the wedding would not be immediate. We were not under any pressure to plan a ceremony, pick a date, or any of the other decisions that typically overwhelm the wedding process. Instead, I was more concerned with where we could move together. Where would we begin our lives as a married couple? He was from "the Region," which is located on the northernmost tip of Indiana near Chicago, whereas I wanted to continue pursuing a career in the performing arts, which would require a move to a big city. Little did I know that this was not the only decision that would make me question my future with Cliff.

I DON'T???

Within weeks, I got a sinking feeling. Or was it cold feet? Whatever it was, I could not explain the overwhelmingly heavy feeling that I was not doing the right thing. Was this the man I was supposed to spend the rest of my life with? I loved Cliff. I still do, but the thought of being married scared me. I thought about all the things I loved about him to justify committing my life to him as his wife. In the same thought, I considered the things I didn't like, which seemed to be magnified by my growing anxiety. If I didn't like the way he chewed his gum, for instance, and he never changed that behavior, would I be okay with that? For life?

Maybe I'm exaggerating. So, what was so frightening about marrying the man who made me feel safe and secure? Why couldn't I just be happy that someone loved me the way he did? He would drop anything he was doing to take care of me and I trusted him wholeheartedly. He valued family and frequently reminded me to mend bridges with them when there was a dispute. Cliff believed life was too short to hold grudges, and that may be why Mom'ela, GMa, and my sister loved him like their own. He had a relationship with each of them and talked to them regularly. If the three people whose opinion I valued the most liked him, what was wrong with me? What was holding me back?

After some thought, I realized my hesitation stemmed from a deeply rooted fear. It was his recreational use of marijuana. Though many people defend the legal use of it for medicinal purposes, I have come to see it as something that caused me much fear. Why? Because as a child, my mother often said that marijuana was the gateway to the other drugs she used, and you see how that unfolded. In my mind, marijuana became cocaine, which led to an uncontrollable addiction that negatively impacted my family. Because of that, I resolved that my future children would not go through it either.

Perhaps more important, I was afraid of myself. My fear

was that I would start the cycle of drug abuse. If marijuana was accessible to me during a stressful time, I was afraid I would start using it to cope. Once that high was not good enough, I feared I would try something else. It may not have been cocaine like my mother, but it could have been another substance.

I waited as long as I could before making a permanent decision. I went back and forth for days trying to avoid making the life-changing decision to move forward or burning this bridge by calling off the engagement. What if I missed out on a great marriage by leaving now? Would Cliff be the one who got away?

After much thought, I finally decided I did not want to move forward with Cliff. I didn't know the best way to tell him so I wrote him a letter. We both had keys to each other's place and I left the letter where he could see it in his apartment. As I write this, I now see how breaking up hurts both people, including the one who decided to leave. Who knows? Maybe fragments of my relationship with Cliff unknowingly foreshadowed my marriage and divorce.

> *"I went from being a happily engaged woman to a damaged single woman who broke the heart of the man who loved me as any woman desires to be loved by a man."*

Cliff was hurt—obviously hurt and confused once he read the letter. Almost immediately after he received it, he drove to my home to make sure it was officially over. We had a brief interaction in my dark apartment, but I don't remember what was said that night. For a short time following, Cliff reached out to me in disbelief but I made myself inaccessible. I tried not to be at home when I knew he would come by. If I answered the phone, I tried to keep the conversation short. Once we exchanged the keys to each other's place, it was clear there was no turning back. In one summer, I went from being a happily engaged woman to a damaged single woman who broke the heart of the man who loved me as any woman desires to be loved by a man.

Because our relationship was deeply rooted in friendship, we remained in contact. Within a year of our breakup, he told me he was expecting his first child. Though I had contemplated giving our relationship another shot, the news of his first-born child stopped any immediate thoughts of reconciliation. When I graduated from undergrad and returned to Indianapolis in December 2006, Cliff soon followed in hopes of being closer to me and that I would reconsider our relationship. What little existed of our friendship dwindled as he received my mixed signals as signs of hope for us. He finally began to give up after I ceased contact with him and shifted more of my focus elsewhere.

CHAPTER 8

CAN YOU SEE (THE REAL) ME?

Fatherless African American women are often perceived as troubled, damaged, and struggling with issues of abandonment, insecurity, and self-esteem.
~Dr. Eunice Matthews-Armstead, Clinical Social Worker/Therapist

GUARDED. I HAD BEEN IN a war and survived and now I was not going to let anything or anyone else hurt me again. My success in high school was due to the mask of strength I wore, and I made it! I graduated and was on the path of becoming the successful woman I always wanted to be. "I am strong!" was my daily mantra and this strength was what society reinforced as well. I became so blinded by my need to be strong that I overlooked the pain harbored inside me. Behind this wall of "strength" was a girl who needed to be loved and not be on the battlefield all the time.

WEARING THE STRONG BLACK WOMAN (SBW) MASK

Cliff fought for me, but what was he fighting against? Why did he have to fight for my love? Why did it take so long for me to let my guard down with him? Why couldn't I be my true self, flaws and all? It was because the true me was hidden behind the disguise I put on years ago. He fought to remove this mask that was affixed to me like the inextricable one Jim Carrey wore in the movie *The Mask*. But the mask I wore is commonly worn by other African American women, including my GMa, Mom'ela, and aunts. These women started wearing the mask after they trusted men with their hearts and resources, only to find themselves disappointed and left alone. This mask served to protect me from being vulnerable with anyone who could break my heart while pushing away the people who may have genuinely loved me. It was the mask of the Strong Black Woman, or SBW.

What does it mean to be a Strong Black Woman? According to clinical psychologists Roxanne Donovan and Lindsey West, the stereotypical SBW mistakes "excessive strength, caregiving, and emotional restraint as central to Black womanhood." In other words, SBWs present themselves as strong when faced with a situation that anyone would find difficult to manage. SBWs often overextend themselves when caring for others. SBWs overlook their emotional needs in favor of who they perceive is a more dominant idea or person. Many women can identify with these traits; however, what distinguishes a SBW from other women is the complexity of her experience in America.

"Imagine the difficulty of letting your guard down when you've had to advocate for yourself in the face of relentless opposition."

In a similar study, entitled, "Young, Black, and Female: The Challenge of Weaving an Identity," the authors defined the social conditions that encourage the SBW ideology. In the study, African American women at a California community college were interviewed to determine which aspects of their identity were most salient. The findings revealed that the most prevalent trait was race, followed by gender. However, the researchers found the trait that was not far behind was strength. They hypothesized that it was necessary for Black women to exude strength in our patriarchal society where racial oppression is prevalent. Imagine the difficulty of letting your guard down when you've had to advocate for yourself in the face of relentless opposition.

By the time I met Cliff, I had been wearing the SBW mask for most of my life. In that time, I learned to accept my father's absence as a normal part of my experience. I hid my hurt behind my accomplishments. A nonchalant response or gesture covered the disappointment I often felt when Dad did not follow through with a promise from his last cameo appearance. In conversations, I'd immediately change the subject to something more positive if someone asked more information about him.

On the surface, it seemed I was strong, but my supposed strength concealed the worry and stress I often experienced because of the challenges I've faced. In college, I believed I could manage going to school full time, working, and taking care of a teenager (I don't see how those of you with teenagers do this) on my own. I could not complain about not having enough money until payday. I could not complain about not having the strength to juggle my many responsibilities. I could not complain about how life was unfair. I had to manage it all and be my own last resort. Though I had assistance, I was my backup plan. I was existing in the world while simultaneously locked inside my own "in case of an emergency break glass" box.

I thought it would take the strength of heavy equipment and mighty power to remove the SBW façade I had maintained. It was the makings of my identity. I appeared to be doing it all unscathed and unaffected by life every time I introduced myself with a smile. On the inside, however, I felt the weight of the world on my shoulders. Let me tell you, appearances are not reality. But it turned out that removing my mask would not require brute strength. Instead, it just took love. Cliff's love for me is all that it took to surrender the SBW idea. His love gave me a safe space to remove my mask.

DAD, CAN YOU TAKE OFF THIS MASK?

During college, one of my deepest needs was to be vulnerable with someone I could trust. To totally express my dreams, nightmares, interests, and not be judged or redirected to something I "should" be doing. I needed to express my fears and doubts authentically without being told I needed to "just deal with it." More than anything, I needed to let go of the weight caused by my life's motto of being a "Strong Black Woman who could do anything I put my mind to" with the neck swirling, "wait a minute" finger lifted, pouted duck-lipped manner that's often associated with the sassy Black woman. I needed to experience the opposite of that ideal, but I didn't know exactly what I needed nor did I know what that looked like.

Everyone in the community could see what "good" I was doing. I was a "good" student in school who did not give my teachers or the administration grief. I was the one who would "make it to college." Once I got to college, I had to learn the ropes of "doing" higher education as a first-generation college student. Not only was I learning how to be a student, but there is much more to college success than academics. Take it from me—I work in higher ed.

My family knew what I had overcome based on what they saw. But they were missing some important pieces of my story that have impacted the choices I now make and with whom I open up to. Even my two best girlfriends from high school, Chrisette and Riley, were surprised to learn intimate details while reading the earlier drafts of this book. Imagine learning more in one year about someone you considered a best friend when you have known them for almost twenty years! That is how good I was able to wear the mask of the SBW.

But I craved a relationship that would allow me to be myself freely. I wanted my father to know me. And I wanted to know more about him beyond what I learned from my mother or the people who know him. According to Psychologist Linda Nielsen, this longing is not uncommon in father-daughter relationships. In a fifteen-year study, she collected data on over four-hundred college women and found that "most daughters want more from the relationship with their father—more comfortable communication, more time together, more emotional sharing, more knowledge of one another." To me, however, it is hard to have this type of relationship with a father who is not reliable or available to establish or maintain this type of connection.

Meaningful connection is important for the father-daughter relationship. In a communications study, Dr. Narissra Punyanunt-Carter expanded Bowlby's theory of attachment to determine how the quality of the father-daughter relationship impacted how they communicated with each other. One of Punyanunt-Carter's findings was that daughters and fathers vary in their motivation for communicating with each other. In particular, the fathers in her study communicated with their daughters regardless of their attachment to her. However, "*anxious/ambivalent* daughters may communicate less for escape motives because they have not achieved a competent or satisfying feeling of escape from past interactions with their fathers." In other words, if the daughter has a meaningful relationship with her father, she is more likely to invest time communicating with him and to rely on their father because he has proven himself to be trustworthy. But daughters who are unsure or on the fence about their relationship with their fathers are less likely to do so.

My relationship with my father remained on a superficial level because of his inconsistency. The disappointment was much like a losing scratch-off lottery ticket. With several scrapes of your coin, it looks like you may get three of a kind or the bonus money, only to find you did not win anything at all.

Until college, the main three things I could tell you about my father was his name, that he was seeing someone, and that he loved Cadillac Sedans. And what did he know about me? Not much at all. What I desired was for him to get to know me, my interests, my middle name even, but it never happened. He never got to know his daughter behind the mask I wore to protect myself from the hurt our relationship caused.

> "For a long time, I mistook my survival for strength, my endurance for resiliency."

UNMASKING THE SBW

During my freshman year of college, I began reading Iyanla Vanzant's *Yesterday, I Cried*, which began my emotional healing process. In it, she is very candid about the hardships she faced and how the tearful experiences helped to develop her. For a long time, I mistook my survival for strength, my endurance for resiliency. I failed to realize I was bleeding, that I was actually weak because I did not acknowledge my woundedness. I was emotionally traumatized like a soldier who endured war. Looking over my shoulder in fear. Taking calculated steps because the next step, choice, or mistake could have fatal consequences.

I felt both alone and as a part of a marginalized group. I did not know anyone who had gone through what I had experienced in my immediate circle but there had to be others who did. Neither my high school friends nor my cousins faced the adversity my sister and I endured. Their biggest challenges seemed to be what to choose from their pool of abundance, but all I had known was insufficiency until I read Iyanla's books. As I read *Yesterday, I Cried*, I cried for who I was yesterday, who

I am today, and was guaranteed to cry for who I will become tomorrow. Finally, I felt, there was someone who understood the depth of my pain and whom I could connect to. Our bond was so tight that I would refer to Iyanla as one of my "other mothers" from afar, but was there someone else in my circle I could open up to? Someone "in my neighborhood" who was more accessible to provide the emotional support I needed?

Reading Iyanla's books peeled away the initial layers of my emotional shell, but Cliff's friendship met this yearning long before we ever entered a romantic relationship. Cliff was the first man to investigate the contents of my heart and to see me as more than a SBW. I had been walking around for years carrying the weight of my life because I did not trust anyone. People were inconsistent. Much of my childhood was filled with empty promises of being rescued.

With one look at my face, however, Cliff could tell something was going on within me. The conversations started with a simple, "How you doing, Shaven?" (Shaven is the nickname he gave me.) I'd lie and say I was fine.

Then he'd ask a follow-up question like, "So, what's really going on?" and cock his head to the side to indicate he knew there was more to the story. He'd gently persist until I finally opened up about the most recent fight with my mother or sister or whatever issue I was wrestling with that day.

My inner struggle would sometimes manifest itself in a physical reaction from me. It was as if the issues I wrestled with internally manifested themselves physically. I'd initiate a wrestling match with Cliff when he asked probing questions, and all he did was let me wear myself out. When I finally surrendered, he'd hug me or console me in such a warm way.

Most important, I learned to trust another human being. Cliff was the first intimate relationship during which I learned to trust a man. In the process, I experienced the fulfillment in letting my guards down. I learned that being vulnerable with the right man will make you feel more feminine and sexy than any talk show makeover or the most expensive sweet-smelling perfume. Being connected with the right person can heal more of your well-being than pretending to be strong all by yourself. And most of all, the emotional healing I received from Cliff occurred before we made our relationship official. Long before we had sex (because I know you're wondering). Cliff truly got me. He saw me.

You will seek me and find me when you seek me with all your heart.
~Jeremiah 29:13

One of my biggest regrets is that Cliff fought against the things within me that he wasn't responsible for causing—the pain of my childhood. He should not have had to battle my lack of trust in men, because he was not the one who broke promises. But Cliff fought for me and knew me in a way I hoped my dad would. I was damaged by my dad's lack of love for me, among other things, and closed off my heart to others, including Cliff. However, I have learned that God often tells us to face the uncomfortable issues of our lives to bring about healing. I would not have understood this had He not used Cliff to demonstrate His love for me. But my healing only took place after I took action, removed my mask, and revealed the contents of my heart.

DIVINE CONTRADICTIONS OF THE HEART

Masking my hurt was also a way of masking the pain in my heart. But I have come to realize that I could not come to God with fragments of my heart and expect Him to heal me. God requires our whole heart. He is able to restore us and to put our pieces back together in ways others cannot. Our family and loved ones' compassion can only go so far, but God can reach the very depths of our pains. He takes us as we are with the expectation that we come to Him to be changed, without masks we wear to protect ourselves.

My first leap of faith as an adult was to take guardianship of my sister. I do not mention this to receive praise or to criticize anyone. But that was one of the scariest decisions I have ever made! On one hand, I was blessed to have Cliff's friendship and support in those early days, but he was not there when I was alone with my thoughts, when it was just me and my fears of raising my sister alone.

It was during this time that I initially learned to come to God with my fears. I had worn the mask of the SBW and its ideologies were reinforced in my mind that even when I took it off and was exposed to Cliff, I still made a backup plan in case he did not follow through. I did the same in my relationship with God. In my mind, I believed in Him, but my behavior often contradicted my belief. Therefore, becoming a guardian at the age of eighteen challenged me to walk by the faith I proclaimed in public and forced me to come to God without a mask of superficial strength.

In Jeremiah 29, Jeremiah wrote to the Jerusalem captives who were captured by Nebuchadnezzar and taken to Babylon. In the letter, Jeremiah shares that God will bring the captives back to their homes. Before He does so, God says He will bless the captives and they would respond by seeking Him with all their heart.

Let me pause here. Imagine hearing from a religious leader or other respected person that God allowed you to be pushed away from a place that represents comfort and stability. It would feel like a slap in the face. Then, before you respond, this person adds that you shouldn't worry because you should still seek

God. How does one do this? How do you seek God with all your heart when He allowed you to go through unpleasant experiences in the first place?

Well, I have come to know that God's way of doing things often contradicts anything that seems humanly reasonable. What if He allowed me to be the daughter of an absent father to demonstrate how He is a father to the fatherless (Psalm 68:5)? What if He allowed Cliff to be a part of my life to show that some men could be trusted? I can only imagine the Jerusalem captives' skepticism when Jeremiah shared his prophesy.

> *"What if He allowed me to be the daughter of an absent father to demonstrate how He is a father to the fatherless (Psalm 68:5)?"*

Another controversial misconception in our healing process is that we must idly wait for it. However, my relationship with Cliff revealed that we must participate in it. I had to be vulnerable about the dark places and shame in order to be free. We cannot be passive and falsely believe that a supernatural healing will simply overtake us. Healing requires our direct energy and effort. Even if we appear to come up short or in deficit, we have to trust that God can go beyond our natural limitations.

My relationship with Cliff was a natural representation of God's supernatural love for us. In both relationships, I had to be a part of my healing process. I had to surrender my pain to God and to seek Him with openness and my whole heart. Cliff may have "wrestled" with me until I opened up to him, but it was up to me to make the choice to be open. Sometimes we wrestle with God when He directs us to do something that's the opposite of what we expected but would bring about healing. We may want to just halt the immediate pain in our hearts, while God asks us to come to Him with all the fragments and pieces of it. How do we do that? I have no elaborate well-thought-out explanation for this other than we must trust God. Plain and simple.

I have come to believe that God allows us to experience things in life that increase our faith in Him, compelling us to lean into the things that make us the most uncomfortable. How could I understand how to trust God like Job if I had not experienced losing "everything"? How could I learn to praise God like the Jerusalem captives in Babylon if I had not been forced to leave the predicament I had accepted as my reality? Today, my praise and prayers are more fervent, having survived the transitions that required uncomfortable faith. I want to encourage you that God loves you and will be there for you when you seek Him wholeheartedly. He expects us to come to Him exposed and uninhibited. Without our masks.

CHAPTER 9

LESSONS IN LOVE

OF THE THREE ROMANTIC RELATIONSHIPS I will highlight, my relationship with Cliff was the most meaningful. He understood that there were many layers to me and spoke to my heart. We were truly friends long before we started dating and that makes a difference in any relationship. Sex can only connect you so far, but a genuine friendship and mutual respect will carry you much further. Even if the relationship between the two of you ends, the impact of it will last a lifetime. The significance of Cliff's love has lasted well beyond our relationship. Unfortunately, he accumulated many scabs and bruises from being the pioneer of my heart. With this in mind, it is with mixed emotions that I share the lessons from our relationship.

IT TAKES MORE THAN LOVE TO LAST A LIFETIME

You can love someone with ALL your heart, but they may not be the person you were destined to be with for a lifetime. I love Cliff. He did everything that I was told men were supposed to do for their lady, and more. If he saw that I needed gas, for instance, he would ask if he could drive my car around the corner and he would turn around within minutes with a full tank of gas. I never had to ask for what I needed. He looked to see where there was a need and would work to meet it. He also took clues from our conversations to meet unspoken needs. It was not that I was being indirect or passive, but remember I was the SBW so I was determined to find a way to fulfill my own needs by any means.

More than anything, I loved how my relationship with Cliff liberated me. Before, I exuded a cheerful attitude and optimism as a coping mechanism. It was as if I wore my happiness as arm flotation devices in the middle of the ocean. My "happy floaters" helped to keep me from sinking immediately, but I still ran the risk of being taken over by the waves of life at any moment. Cliff's love, however, allowed me to walk the beaches of life and enjoy the sand between my toes. Not only did it please him to make me happy, but I was actually happy with myself. I learned to get out of my head and embrace spontaneity. There were remnants of the old me that still had a plan and a long to-do list, but now I was more open to embracing random moments in life. With all the good that came from our relationship, why did it not work?

Part of my reasoning for parting ways was rooted in my spiritual expectations for a long-term relationship. Because I had spent most of my life connected to the church in one way or another, I wanted to connect with a man who could be a spiritual leader in my home. I desired a husband whose vision and direction for our family I could trust. I had to be able to answer at least two questions before considering a lifelong partner. Where would he lead our family? Did I believe in his vision for us?

When Cliff and I were together, he was still trying to find his path. He was not sure of his next steps in life and I knew there was nothing I could do to "set" him on the right track. My attempts to keep my mom from using drugs had failed time and time again. My attempts to motivate my sister to follow in my footsteps had failed as well. So I knew I could not change Cliff. His change and his vision had to come from within. I could inspire him with my life, but any meaningful change had to start from within him.

To answer my own questions, I don't believe we were meant to be together for a lifetime and that is okay. If you are in a relationship with someone—friend, romantic, professional, or otherwise—you must weigh both the pros and cons to see if it is in line with your purpose. Every relationship is not meant to go beyond its peak season. Every man will not be your prince charming. There are a lot of great men, but they may not be the man God has destined for you. You must seek God's guidance before you invest in long-tern relationships. He will answer your prayers for clarity, but it is also important not to ignore Him when He reveals the answer. Sometimes we want things to work out rather than trusting God's "no." Ultimately, His ways are better than ours.

EMBRACE RELATIONSHIPS (SELF) REVELATIONS

Another lesson in love is that relationships have a way of bringing out the best and worst in us. Ask anyone who has been in a long-term relationship—one of the most frustrating things it usually reveals is the not-so-pretty parts of you and your personality. Who likes to be told they are not as perfect as they thought? I would imagine the answer is no one, but our relationships have the power of equalizing us with the person we are connected to. Once we enter into relationships, they can reveal our selfishness. They reveal our insecurities. Being in a relationship with our partner can illuminate the things we were not ready to deal with if we did not have to. Maybe we considered taking some of our "stuff" to the grave, never to be found out by anyone but God.

One of the biggest lessons I learned about myself while in relationship with Cliff is that I took most of the damage from my childhood into my adulthood. I thought I could go on forever wearing the mask of the SBW. I was afraid of my heart being trampled on, misused, and abused. As a child, I was promised so many things that did not come to pass. With each broken promise, I determined in my heart that I would not make promises I couldn't keep. After living that way for a few years, I realized even *I* could break promises so then I stopped making promises altogether. Instead, I resolved to be a woman of action and adopted the mindset of speaking things aloud only after I had followed through with them.

The hurt caused by broken promises created the layers in the mask I wore and I promised I would not allow myself to be hurt again. People continued making promises and each unfulfilled vow increased my level of skepticism. I could not count how many times I've heard people say they would rescue my sister and I from what was happening at home. They did so in the short-term, but these escapes didn't last longer than a few weekends. This continued until my ears went deaf at the sound of a promise coming from the mere movement of another's mouth. I would not even give their words a chance to permeate my body. I just assumed they would not follow through on their word and I planned for the worst. By the time I met Cliff, I had become accustomed to the myth that I was the only one who could do for me what needed to be done. I felt he was just another person who would let me down and disappoint me. However, he taught me to let my guard down and to learn to trust again.

But before this change came, I fought against what our relationship revealed about me. I did not like hearing I was a perfectionist who required everyone to behave in a controlled manner in my presence. I did not enjoy someone seeing I was not always okay. No one was ever supposed to know I had moments of weakness from trying to manage everything. The sting of hearing the truth from Cliff hit me and caused me to wrestle with him both physically and mentally because I was in denial. At the same time, it caused an inner grappling between my old self and the new self that was emerging. The old me was rigid, but this new me was more liberated and embraced spontaneity. After we broke up, this was one trait I missed most about our relationship—I missed having someone who would challenge me to be more of myself.

After Cliff, I would return to wearing the mask of the Strong Black Woman. I didn't put the entire mask on. I had become somewhat open and changed due to the emotional work I did while in the relationship. However, the mask remained until the events surrounding my divorce opened me up in a new way. Being abandoned by the man I married left me so vulnerable that I had no other option but to tell my truth. I could no longer pretend that I was doing well, because I was not. Neither did I want to pretend. I didn't want to be stronger for anyone else, especially because I did not have strength for myself. Though I will go more in-depth about these events later, I wish I could have experienced that level of vulnerability with another human being even after my relationship with Cliff ended.

SUSTAINING CHANGE

My ability to be vulnerable lasted as long as Cliff and I were in a relationship. Once our relationship was over, my old coping mechanisms returned. They may not have been at the same magnitude, but they returned nevertheless. I hid my true feelings because I did not feel I could trust anyone. Mom'ela often relied on my "strength" to help our family and to serve her needs. She rarely had those in-depth conversations with me like I had with others outside our family of three. Thus, I distanced myself from her emotionally, which caused her to feel that I had no loyalty to her and my sister. My GMa was supportive but was known for encouraging you at the beginning of a conversation, then cursing you out by the end. My sister was still trying to find her way and her perspective on life seemed more defeated than helpful.

I needed to be surrounded by people who would allow me to be myself without expectations. It's hard to trust anyone when the people who are the closest to you expect you to be strong and keep everything together. Letting go of Cliff meant more than just breaking his heart. It also meant I lost the one person who understood me on a deep emotional level.

Change is good. Positive changes in our behavior are great! But if the changes go unnourished and underdeveloped, then we return to old behaviors and our former ways of coping with life. The Bible informs us that transforming ourselves involves a change in how we think and we must continue renewing our minds (Romans 12:2). It also reminds us that if we continue to be our old selves and act out of old behaviors, we'll continue to grow in dishonorable ways. To change, we must renew our minds to become more like the people God created us to be (Ephesians 4:20-24).

> *"Instead, I was more like the children of Egypt who found it easier to look BACK on their bondage than to look FORWARD to God's promises."*

To solidify the change that was happening within me, I needed to continue renewing my mind. I needed to continue seeking God to do the work He had already began within me. Instead, I was more like the children of Egypt who found it easier to look BACK on their bondage than to look FORWARD to God's promises. I still focused on what seemed the most beneficial about wearing the SBW mask and failed to see a new way of doing things. I failed to practice telling my truth whether it was welcomed or not. I continued to hide and only sometimes share how I felt if someone asked, but even then I did not trust they really cared and I judged their motives to determine whether I should really open up. One look away during a conversation or one interruption would cause me to close up and withdraw from the emotional sharing in an instant. I felt that whomever was worthwhile to hear the nature of my heart had to do so without any distractions. Period.

Now, almost ten years later, I am pressing toward a new way of doing things, but you do not have to wait as long to do so. I encourage you to go the way God is directing you. It will not feel comfortable. Things will appear to be better in your past than they are in this very moment. But unless you keep pressing forward, true change cannot occur. You will continue to go through the cycle you are currently experiencing. You will continue to attract the same type of romantic partners you've always attracted. If you have ever done a Jillian Michaels workout, you know that she is crazy! But she also says, "Get comfortable with being uncomfortable," and this is so true for choosing a new direction in your life.

> *"It is critical to trust God and lean into what seems uncomfortable as you tread the new path before you."*

Whatever God is leading you through as you are reading this, follow His way. His way is perfect. He will not fail you. He will be with you through your journey and meet you on the road with opportunities designed just for you if you just trust Him. Believe me. I had no other choice but to trust Him throughout the writing and healing process. Likewise, whenever you experience a shift in your life it is critical to trust God and lean into what seems uncomfortable as you tread the new path before you.

Though I have much love and appreciation for Cliff, he was not what I was looking for in a long-term relationship. At the time, he met only part of what it took to be my ideal partner while also being more than I realized I needed. I didn't realize I needed to be loved in the way he loved me, but Cliff was just the "sweats" to my "suit and sweats" expectations for a man. What came next was the guy in the suit, but the relationship was a walk on the wild side. Addictive, if you will, but I won't spoil it. You'll just have to turn the page to learn more about Leo.

LEO:
Dating Daddy's Substitute

Shavonne was very active in undergrad which led her to being nominated and selected for membership in the Mortar Board National Honor Society. She would serve as her class' president for the organization. Pictured here with longtime adviser Barbara Cook.

CHAPTER 10

"AGE AIN'T NOTHING BUT A NUMBER"

AS SOON AS I MOVED in with my dad during the summer of 2006, I applied to multiple jobs in a shopping mall where I had previously worked. Waiting was an exhaustive process but within a few weeks, I interviewed and accepted the first part-time job offer. By June, I was working two retail positions in fashion and a third in a kiosk that sold cellular phones. Working in the mall not only helped me to make some income, but it was also the place where my father's lessons played out. I learned firsthand some critical life lessons about relationships through the men I met that epic summer of 2006.

NUMBER ONE WITH A BULLET???

I drew an abundance of male attention working at the kiosk that summer. Men from all backgrounds and professions introduced themselves to try to win a date with me off the clock. It was difficult declining some of the offers because each one was a new adventure. One man, for instance, worked at the movie theatre located a level above my kiosk. I enjoyed going behind the scenes and watching him operate the large rolls of film between movies. Another was from India and he was the operator for a restaurant in the food court. He brought me lunch and gave me large sums of cash as a gift even after I refused. I never asked him for money, but it was clear he was trying to bait me with what he had. It did not work. My dad's daily male-bashing messages rang in my head while on my way to work, but that did not stop me from accepting some of the dates I was offered.

One man particularly caught my attention during a slow closing shift at the kiosk. That evening, I noticed this tall, chocolate skinned gentleman wearing a well-tailored suit that revealed a slender yet muscular physique walking in my direction toward the food court. He later said that he noticed me first and made his way to introduce himself. His name was Leo and I cannot remember the exact nature of our exchange, but his maturity and charisma beguiled me. Leo generally described his profession as he slid me his business card. At the tender age of twenty-one, I was oblivious to his advances like Eve was to the serpent in the Garden of Eden. My naïveté led me to believe he wanted to connect professionally because I had a personal interest in the financial services his company provided. Instead, this would be the beginning of one of the most seductive and disorienting rollercoasters of my life!

Remember I wanted a man who could switch from a suit to sweats seamlessly? Well, Leo was a suits man.

The ride began when I first met Leo for a meal, which was a fascinating yet unsettling experience. I was mesmerized, anxious to meet up with him as soon as he extended the offer. So why do I say unsettling? It most certainly was not his physical appearance because he was GQ fine! He could attract a blind woman from the other side of the planet with his allure and distinct stature! Did I forget to mention that he was fine?

What was somewhat disturbing was something he said during our convo. I shared that I was wrapping up my final semester of undergrad and planned to graduate that December. When he asked about my goals, I told him about my aspirations of becoming a performing artist and my plans to move out of state after graduation. He talked about his days as a student at another large public university in the Midwest and his involvement with his fraternity. By now, I had joined the sorority I was interested in while praising dancing and we connected over the history of the organizations we were a part of. We talked about the high schools we attended and realized they were in the same district, the significance of which is that both of our schools were considered low-performing schools due to the negative stereotype of the district. Yet, both of us persisted through college and were destined for success. He, having already earned a bachelor's degree, had a successful career in finance for several years. Meanwhile, I was on my way to conquering the world once I completed my last semester.

In that moment, our conversation shifted from lighthearted to peculiar. Following the discussion about our dreams, goals, and achievements, he said, "You're number one with a bullet."

Hold up! Was he trying to take my life?

I never thought I would die by a gun, but I began to contemplate my fate and if I made the right choice in accepting his offer for this date.

Why would he say something like that to me??

He must have seen the fear on my face because he promptly explained that the phrase was used to describe an artist's fast move to the top of the Billboard charts. That he could see I would achieve great things and this was only the beginning of that journey. I became more relaxed following his explanation, but there was no denying that what he said as a compliment scared the living daylights out of me! We continued dating that summer until I returned to campus to complete my final semester of undergrad.

A WHOLE NEW WORLD

Once I graduated and returned to Indianapolis in January 2007, Leo and I reunited. Our fling was much like the song in the movie *Aladdin* in that he exposed me to places and things I had never experienced before. For instance, we dined in some of the most underrated and overlooked local restaurants in Indy. My favorite evening with Leo was spent at a quaint little Italian restaurant that was in a charming village-type area of town called Broad Ripple. Anyone who knows me can attest that I am a t-shirt, jeans, and flat shoes type of gal, but Leo asked me to dress up for this evening. Because I was living with a friend from college, Christyn, and her family, I would often visit Leo at his apartment. On that particular evening, I remember the look of amazement on his face when he greeted me at the door. It was the first time he saw me in stilettoes and the look on his face said, "This is going to be a good evening." And so it was.

Leo was and still is a socialite. From the beginning, I knew he was older than me based on the experiences he shared with me, but he did not appear much older than me. He had debonair taste, quality, and style that was not present in any of the men of my generation. Yet he was knowledgeable about contemporary trends and could use popular terminology in its proper context. His swag was classic. His approach was impeccable. Despite his charm, though, part of me was curious about his actual age. When I inquired, he said that he was thirty-five years old, which made him thirteen years my senior.

Eh…that's not TOO bad…

Leo's taste in music became something we bonded over. He listened to everything from old school rhythm and blues to hip hop and contemporary neo soul. We would spend evenings together just listening to tunes he considered contemporary music of his time and I considered as "old school classics." Leo would grin as I sang along to the lyrics of songs from the 1970s while I would laugh as he spat bars from Biggie. I preferred Pac. Nonetheless, he expanded my taste in music by exposing me to artists that were not regularly played on the radio. His collection included music from Solange, pre-the phenomenon known as *A Seat at the Table*, to jazz artists whose music was as calming as a cool evening breeze through the front window. Leo knew how to set the mood whether we were relaxing at his place or preparing for a night of entertainment out on the town.

As he was in the shower preparing for an evening out, I saw Leo's driver's license. When I looked at the date of birth and did some math, I thought I calculated the wrong number. Leo told me that he was thirty-five, but my math indicated he was actually forty years old! When I realized there was an eighteen-year age gap between us, my thoughts spun out of control. He was a few years younger than my mother and I realized I could have been his child.

I was born a month after he would have graduated from high school!

Shocked, I waited for Leo to get out of the shower before confronting him about my discovery. He seemed embarrassed about me learning the truth. I was not bothered by his age as much as I was upset by his lie. I could have ended it all there, but I didn't and we went on the date as planned.

Yet, on the inside I tried to make meaning of it and why I chose to be involved with a man who was almost the same age as my dad. No matter how hard I attempted to overlook our age difference, I began questioning my relationship with Leo.

Was I acting out the infamous "daddy issues" by dating Leo?

Or was I just drawn to an attractive man whom I connected with through shared interests?

No matter how hard I tried, I could not justify my connection with Leo even when it became clear that it was an unhealthy one. God Himself revealed to me that I did not have a future with this charismatic Casanova.

MEETING AT THE WELL

God may have sent me signals from the beginning that I should not be connected with Leo. It began with subliminal clues or hints that made me uncomfortable. Leo was inconsistent and unclear in his messaging. For instance, he would send random and often cryptic text messages that even I could not understand.

"Hey"

"I miss you Baby"

"Wya" or "where ya at?"

But one of the more obvious clues was when I attempted to let go of Leo and he responded with stalker-like behaviors. When I lived in my first studio apartment on the ground floor, he would knock on the door in the middle of the night uninvited. When I did not answer the door, he would knock on the window, which was frightening. I would try to remain as silent as possible to avoid being heard and unmovable to avoid being seen by him when he'd peer through the window. As a result, I vowed to never live on the ground floor if I could avoid it. Unfortunately, the inconsistency in my resolve caused me to reconnect with him and continue the on and off cycle for what would become four years.

Even if I were to give in to his advances, did we really have a future together? We were at two opposing points in our lives. I wanted to establish a career, purchase my first home, get married and begin my own family, whereas he was well into his career, had owned several homes, been married and divorced, and already had four children of his own—two of them were under the age of eighteen. Leo had his two younger children every other weekend. If I didn't already feel self-conscious about our age difference, his youngest children served as reminders.

Not only did they want to hang out with me like a peer, but I became affectionately known as "teenager" by them. Talk about awkward!

My heart became convinced I needed to change once I returned to seeking God's guidance by returning to church. Have you ever attended a church service and felt as if the minister was preaching directly to you about your unique situation? Well, that is exactly what happened to me almost every Sunday I was in the house of worship. It was as if the minister had visited my home, learned the intimate details of my life, and shared the secrets during the service in front of hundreds of people. I didn't attend church regularly, but when I did the message typically included biblical warnings against fornication after I was intimate with Leo. How ironic! Or was God trying to tell me something?

Other sermons addressed the importance of being whole before seeking a long-term relationship. In my mind, I was complete because I used my career status and growing independence to measure my development and wholeness. My, was I wrong! There was a need within me that this relationship was meeting but I was unclear as to what it was.

Feelings of "post-intimacy guilt" would follow me home. After we were intimate, I would go to the edge of the bed and pray for God to forgive me. I prayed for Him to comfort me with His Word and deliver me. Then I would open the Bible near the bed, randomly pick a spot and read. But when I opened the Bible after my prayer of conviction, the first verse I'd read addressed fornication! I could not believe this, but then it would happen every time I repeated the cycle. Now, there was no denying that God was trying to tell me something! The routine was: Leo and I would be intimate, I'd feel guilty, pray, open the Bible, and "thou shall not fornicate" messages would be the first thing I read every time from different chapters in the Bible! I had to "bump my head" several times, but God's Word was clear and it was no coincidence I was supposed to hear Him in that way.

Finally, during my private time with God, He began to show me revelations about the Samaritan woman at the well in John 4. When she met Jesus, it appears as if He was in need because He asked the woman for a drink. Instead, this was an opportunity for Jesus to fill the woman's deepest needs. In John 4:13-14, Jesus answered, "Everyone who drinks this water will be thirsty again, but whoever drinks the water I give them will never thirst. Indeed, the water I give them will become in them a spring of water welling up to eternal life." After meditating on this verse and the story, I began questioning if Jesus would be all that I needed. Could He meet the deepest longings and desires that I had within? As this point in my life, I was seeking validation from my relationship with Leo, but this story piqued my curiosity and ignited the beginning of a spiritual paradigm shift.

> *"I was beyond nervous to leave the thing I found comfort in but I knew this relationship did not align with my purpose."*

I felt the verses toward the end of her encounter with Jesus were a call to action for both the Samaritan woman and me. After Jesus ministered to the woman at the well, He commanded her to retrieve her husband and return to Him. When she stated that she did not have a husband, Jesus responded in John 4:18, "The fact is, you have had five husbands, and the man you now have is not your husband. What you have just said is quite true." Jesus knew the woman was connected to a man who was not her husband just like He knew Leo was not mine. He knew the Samaritan woman's history and that I had failed relationships with men as well. There are many lessons to be gleaned from the "well" experience, but at that point in my life, I believe God was telling me that He was all I needed and it was vital to let go of Leo. As I began the process of seriously packing my bags on my relationship with Leo, I was beyond nervous to leave the thing I found comfort in but I knew this relationship did not align with my purpose.

...AS THE TABLES TURN

As they say, it is a process to develop a habit and it is a process to change them. Leo and I were connected for three years before I realized I seriously needed to move on, and it was a journey to let him go. As I was coming to terms with what God shared with me about the Samaritan woman, I continued visiting Leo and communicating with him by phone, but this occurred less frequently. Then he would send a text in the middle of the night:

"Hey"

Sometimes I would respond. Other times, I was reminded of the Samaritan woman and I'd roll over in my bed to spend the evening alone in my apartment. This weaning-off process was frightening because I had come so accustomed to the comforts of our relationship. I was used to the sound sleep I'd get when he spent the night at my apartment. When I returned to sleeping alone, however, every creak and sound in my new apartment, on the third floor, was audible in the night, making it hard to get sufficient rest.

Do you remember that Leo had a history of stalking me when I initially tried to break things off with him? Well, now the tables had turned! Following the "woman at the well" revelation in 2009, Leo also grew distant, which led me to seek his attention in the same way he sought me out before—by stalking him. I am ashamed to admit that I had stooped so low, but the energy between us shifted. His distance drew me to obsession. Obsessed to see him. Obsessed to hear his voice. Obsessed to feel his embrace one last time. When he became inaccessible by phone, I began driving past his home only to find he was not there. Eventually, he returned my calls but the messages were brief and sounded cryptic. It was as if Leo was always in the middle of a big case and was just one clue away from solving the crime. He spoke in code. It reminded me of my mother's tone when she was high and was hard to understand. It was very choppy. I did not have a clue what was going on in his world, but the cryptic messaging was starting to get old to me. I took it as a sign to cut the tie for the last time.

Because I was trying to end the relationship with Leo, I didn't realize he was actually in trouble. He contacted me after midnight on several occasions to see if he could spend the night. It did not help that he had a history of calling wolf to draw me in numerous times before, but I refused to submit to him this time. I knew the issue was more serious when the calls decreased in their frequency over a short time until Leo ceased calling me altogether. On one hand, I was relieved, but I was still concerned about Leo's well-being.

This time when I went to check on him, it was out of concern and not out of obsession. I would drive by his place of employment and residence if they were within the vicinity of my destination. Leo's job was in a high traffic area and the building included a large window, which made his desk visible. When he was at work, he looked as if all was well with him. But how could he be doing well if he just sounded desperate in his last voicemail or text? His home that I spent much time in was on a one-way street and I would drive by slowly to see if there was any sign of life in the house. I cannot remember a time when it appeared like someone was in the house. When I finally gathered the nerve to knock on the door months later, I found there was a new family living there.

Embarrassed, I began to shift my focus back to God and His lessons from my well experience. I needed to focus on following Him and improving my own life, which meant I needed to permanently let go of Leo. I needed to let God take care of Leo instead of trying to help a wounded person while I was broken. It was a slow process that began long before I ceased all communication with Leo. But by early spring 2010, the chase ended.

CHAPTER 11

NATURE OF THE CHASE

THE FIRST TWO YEARS OF knowing Leo, he pursued me like a cheetah chasing a gazelle. He especially ran quicker to stay connected when I attempted to distance myself from him, but at some point things changed. The nature of the chase shifted from the cheetah stalking me to this gazelle chasing after him. The prey became the predator. I found my interest in him both intoxicatingly necessary and unexplainable. Nothing in me could describe why I was attracted to him to that magnitude. To find the answers I needed, I decided to investigate relationships like ours. That way, I could learn more about my own motivations that seemed so mysterious even to me.

UNDERSTANDING AGE DISPARITIES IN DATING

Why do some women prefer men who are old enough to be their fathers? What came to mind were obvious reasons including financial gain and physical attraction. But I wanted to go deeper. I wanted to learn more about the psychological and emotional needs of a woman who chooses to date an older man.

According to Clinical Psychologist Vinita Mehta, the phenomenon in which older men prefer dating younger women and vice versa is known as the age differential effect. At first, I had a difficult time finding data on the age differential effect in America beyond quantitative studies. But my questions could not be answered with numbers; I needed to know the "why." When I expanded my search beyond the United States, I was able to find studies that scratched the surface of my curiosity.

My first discovery was that social and cultural norms shape age disparities in romantic relationships. In other words, it may be culturally acceptable for women to marry men who are almost twice their age in one part of the world than in another. In a study of age variations among couples in developing countries, social demographers John Casterline, Lindy Williams, and Peter McDonald analyzed data from the World Fertility Survey in five global regions. Of the twenty-nine countries surveyed, women were on average five years younger than their husbands, but Sub-Saharan Africa had the highest percentage of marriages with fifteen or more years between the wife and husband. According to the scholars, in regions where polygyny was acceptable, the men often had additional wives who were exceptionally younger.

Another realization was that women tend to determine the parameters of the dating pool. Women set the standards for the age difference between them and their significant other simply by making the choice to date particular men—which usually limits the number of available men. In a study of dating preferences using online dating advertisements, psychologists Michael J. Dunn, Stacey Brinton, and Lara Clark explain that men have an idea of their age requirements for short-term relationships, which includes women increasingly younger than themselves, whereas women are more likely to prefer men their age or somewhat older in long-term relationships.

Similar conclusions were found in the study, "Women's and Men's Sexual Preferences and Activities with Respect to the Partner's Age: Evidence for Female Choice" that surveyed over 12,000 Finnish women and men. In this study, the researchers found that the women were more likely to be sexually interested in and involved with men who were within a couple of years their age, whereas many of the men reported being sexually involved with women closer to their age despite their preference for younger women. Interestingly, there was an inconsistency between the man's interest in younger women and his actual involvement with women closer to his age. The researchers reasoned that this may be due to younger women, who were of the age the men preferred, chose to date men within three to five years of them. But was this true in America? With this new understanding of how cultural norms shape dating trends, I decided to adjust my search again.

What I found was a plethora of celebrity scandals involving relationships with significant age disparities. When it comes to those involving minors, in particular, these relationships are obviously frowned upon more than those relationships where the individuals involved are considered adults. For instance, not many people bat an eye at the twelve-year age difference between our beloved Beyoncé and Jay Z or the couple formerly known as "Brangelina" between Angelina Jolie and Brad Pitt. However, R&B crooner R. Kelly has yet to redeem his character from his marriage to budding singer Aaliyah when she was fifteen years old and he was twenty-seven. It does not help that he has endured several subsequent claims against him of inappropriate relationships with minors. Still, the age disparity in these relationships seems small compared to the thirty-four-year difference between *The Green Mile* star Doug Hutchison and his wife Courtney Stodden. He was fifty years old when he married Courtney at the tender age of sixteen.

Leo and I were somewhere in the middle and despite the eighteen-year age difference, he was young at heart. He was like an antique car on display next to the latest model vehicles at an auto show. Though the newer models were equipped with the latest gadgets, Leo was in mint condition with no signs of slowing down. Still, there are at least two themes that come to mind when there is a relationship between two people with an age disparity like ours. First, there is the...

SUGAR DADDY & GOLD DIGGER

Social Demographer Nancy Luke describes the "sugar daddy" as "an adult male who exchanges large amounts of money or gifts for sexual favors from a much younger woman." In her study, Luke collected data from men in an area in Sub-Saharan Africa who were older than their sexual partners by ten years or more and have made significant financial contributions to them. She presumed the relationships involving sugar daddies were less likely to practice safe sex including the use of condoms. Among her findings was that the women were less effective in negotiating safe sex if there is an economic gap between her and her partner. Due to their powerlessness, it would appear that women were forced to be silent by their sugar daddies.

On the other hand, we consider the woman who is linked to a sugar daddy as a "gold digger." A gold digger, according to Psychologist Jasmine N. Ross, is "a woman who uses her sexuality to enter into a relationship (often marriage) with a man primarily for the purposes of attaining a higher socio-economic status." In other words, sex is used as capital in exchange for a sense of security or to attain and maintain a particular status in life. And of course, both men and women can be sugar daddies (or mamas) and gold diggers. According to Ross, the hip hop culture propagates the negative stereotypes of African American women as the gold digger. Rapper Kanye West made a hit song off this very concept! So, imagine the stigma and negative assumptions about women involved with older men even if they sought the relationship out of love.

Let's make this clear: Leo was not my sugar daddy nor was I

a gold digger. It could appear as if I was in his pockets because he worked in finance, but I never asked him for money. Not one dime. At that point in my life, between the ages of twenty-two and twenty-six, I wanted to establish myself, for myself. Though I had needs and robbed Peter to pay Paul, I did not want to supplicate him for assistance in fear that he would think I was at his beck and call. And there is no worse feeling than the guilt of being indebted to someone because they gave you even the slightest amount of assistance in a moment of desperation. My GMa, aunts, and mother did not raise me to rely on a man financially. Instead, they taught me to demand respect of them by obtaining and maintaining independence.

This is not to say Leo and I did not have an exchange of sorts. Our relationship met my need for intimacy while meeting his need for temporary connectivity. Leo was a socialite who chased the next high-end event or executive affair in our city and throughout the country. His closet was filled with suits, ties, and shoes for every occasion and he wore every piece well. Yet it was in the still moments of each other's company I realized he was alone. Undeniably alone. There was an air of desolation about him. An internal cavity that could not be filled by any black-tie gathering, soirée, or my company, which made for a precarious relationship between us.

On the other hand, I gained fulfillment through our in-depth conversations. Leo helped me understand the value of unconditional love for one's family through the stories he shared about forgiveness. He'd reiterate that I needed to learn how to forgive my immediate family, especially when their hurtful actions in the present triggered bad memories and hurt. And even amid our imperfect relationship, Leo and I had conversations about God and the Bible.

I believe Leo understood my emotional needs and knew how

the ending of our relationship affected me. Like a sugar daddy, Leo leveraged his resources to his benefit. Instead of money, he manipulated me for his own sexual and emotional needs when I thought we were on the same playing field. Once I became aware of the imbalance, I realized he contacted me at times it was most convenient for him, like between the hours of ten in the evening when I was in bed until five in the morning before he would get ready for work. It would almost always start with a text:

> *"A woman who dates a man who is significantly older is looking for a substitute for her father."*

"Hey" or
"Wya"

When I did give in to his requests to meet up, we would either have a passionate evening of romance or unwind to music before going to bed in each other's arms.

DATING DADDY'S SUBSTITUTE

Besides the stereotypical sugar daddy and gold digger roles, another prevalent theme is that the relationship signals some unmet need the woman has from their childhood. In discussing the effects of absent fathers on their daughters, Secunda states that a woman who dates a man who is significantly older is looking for a substitute for her father. If a substitute is someone or something that stands in for the real thing, what would I want from Leo that I did not get from my biological father?

What I've come to learn is that clarity about a situation can come from inquiring about what is missing or intangible. In the process of writing this memoir, some of my old beliefs surfaced. I realized there were some harmful beliefs such as the Strong Black Woman concept that have both benefitted my progress and inhibited my ability to connect with others. While looking at the scholarship, opinions, and commentary behind various relationship dynamics, I was able to debunk some of the myths I once held tightly as truths. I uncovered things I did not have the language for when I was younger. I made connections between what I read and heard to my own lived experience, all because I sought the answers to questions about obscure factors in the relationships.

So, as I did some soul searching to make meaning of the idea of dating an older man for a substitute father, I began to ponder what Leo and I did when we were not physical. Music! Music immediately came to mind. We listened to feel-good music regularly. Visual arts. We painted in his kitchen as well as admired the works of fine artists and photographers. Dreams. We talked about our dreams, goals, and next steps in life. And in thinking about our ambitious conversations, I made the connection! It became clear how he served as a substitute for my biological father.

> *"What would I want from Leo that I did not get from my biological father?"*

From the moment we met at the kiosk in the mall, I was able to have the conversations with him that a daughter would have with her daddy. Like my own father, Leo gave me advice but it was not about how "brothers ain't it" or about the "dumb stuff men do." What Leo had to offer that distinguished him from my father, mentors, and any man I could have dated who was my contemporary was that I could talk to him about the full picture and benefit from his experienced perspective. A mentor may have known the superficial details about the decisions I contemplated, but wouldn't always know the complexities of the motivation behind the decision. A man my age may have listened to me, but would lack the forethought Leo offered. Like a father, Leo had enough life experience and wisdom to understand the consequences for the choices I shared with him.

I learned a lot from Leo. And while in the process of learning I also realized how foolish it was to think we would have a future together. Leo's kids were closer to my age than I was to his. I wanted to start a family of my own but I doubted he wanted more children. Though he served as a "substitute" father to me, and I say that loosely, he would never be the father to my children. He would never meet my deepest needs like Jesus could. Once I realized that, it was easier to create the distance needed to move on.

THIRST NO MORE

> *Jesus answered and said to her, "Whoever drinks of this water will thirst again, but whoever drinks of the water that I shall give him will never thirst. But the water that I shall give him will become in him a fountain of water springing up into everlasting life.*
> ~John 4:13-14

Though Jesus referred to the well water as a temporary fix, I also see this passage applying to the use of romantic relationships to quench our deepest thirst. If we're not careful, we will connect with people who are forever bound to us. In the church, we refer to this as "soul ties." These are the strong connections forged between partners once physical intimacy is involved. During sex, there is a supernatural exchange that occurs in which part of their spirit is left with us while a part of ours is left with them.

We can get so caught up in the pleasure that comes from sex that we lose the purpose, meaning, and value in it. Sex can become a coping mechanism for us if we are not careful. It can impair our ability to see things clearly or even hide our deepest unresolved issues. I was so blinded by my attraction to Leo that I lost the ability to see the relationship for what it really was. I now realize the true nature of our bond and how sex was used as a bargaining tool to have our needs met. In the end, there was never enough sex that could meet my emotional needs, nor his. It would have never been enough to quench our bottomless appetites. Unfortunately, our patriarchal society excuses men for their promiscuity while denouncing women for theirs.

Oftentimes, women get criticized for dating a man with means and they are often labeled as "thirsty." However, my thirst was for a more intimate relationship with my biological father. I longed for the conversations that would give me direction in life. I longed to be validated beyond my physical beauty. I longed to be known on a more intimate level by the man who I assumed would fight to get to know me as his daughter. Instead, I found a fix in Leo that provided temporary comfort.

So instead of being a gold digger, I'd say that I was digging on a level that was not as visible to the naked eye. I was seeking to fill the missing parts of my soul. I was looking to meet my spiritual longings by the validation received from romance. Especially from my relationship with Leo. In the beginning, he affirmed what I already knew about myself and my worth. But his seasoned perspective provided a glimpse into what my life could become.

Like a daughter, I wanted to achieve some of the opulence I saw modeled by my father or, in this case, his substitute, Leo. It is similar to the feeling of a father who allows you to sit on Daddy's lap long before you are old enough to drive and pretends you're steering the wheel when actually he's in control. You get to see things from a different point of view. Similarly, Leo introduced me to life outside of my current status as a recent first-generation college graduate in the early stages of my career. Unfortunately, Leo and I were at different points in our lives, which meant there were needs that could not be filled by our connection.

Simply put, Jesus met me at the well during my season with Leo. For as long as I could remember, He was constantly a part of my life. But it was during this time that He reminded me of who He was. He has always filled me in ways the people in my life could not. Leo would never be able to reach me in the places that Jesus resided. Hands down, Leo's inconsistency was unmatched to Jesus's faithfulness.

As with the Samaritan woman, Jesus will meet you on your journey despite your background. The encounter at the well is a demonstration of this as well as how His fulfillment crosses cultural boundaries and is available despite one's circumstances at home. Culturally, Jesus was not supposed to interact with the Samaritan woman, but He did. After she met Him, she changed directions. Instead of returning home, she took a detour into the city to tell others about Jesus, who revealed to her things about herself, and led others to Him.

So here I am. My life has taken an unexpected detour and my hope is to be authentic about my imperfect journey. This book is a testament of God's love and work through me. That includes sharing this relationship that I was in denial about for so long. I was too ashamed to tell many people details about Leo, including my mother who is three years older than him. I couldn't tell my dad because he would have just given one of his "brothers ain't it" speeches right before a date with Leo in our early days. Riley, my friend from high school, would be the only person who would meet him face to face. Other than that, not many people knew of Leo while we were involved with each other. But God knew all the details of this relationship. He knew my deepest desires and met me in the midst of my desperation. He reminded me that a relationship with Him would be the only thing that could fill me. So, I chose Him even while I was afraid of being alone.

CHAPTER 12

WORD TO THE WISE

LEO TAUGHT ME MUCH ABOUT how to progress in my personal and professional relationships. I became more compassionate toward my family and thrived professionally from the insight he provided early in my career. He believed I was capable of achieving much more than I have already achieved. Leo gave me a taste of what my future held and aroused my desire for the finer things in life. Due to the nature of our relationship, however, he did not teach me much about sustaining a lifelong relationship. Instead, my relationship with him taught me to be more vigilant about advances from men, how to set clear boundaries with them, and the value of God's wisdom in setting the guidelines for relationships.

READ BETWEEN THE LINES

One of the biggest lessons Leo taught me was to read between the lines. As mentioned, there was an air of mystique about him and I learned there is often more to the communication than what is being said or sent in a message. Initially, I was flattered when I would hear "I want to see you," but that was only the first half of a full statement. An "I want to see you" text in the middle of the night may mean, "I do not want to be alone tonight" or "I want to be physically intimate with you." Generally speaking, someone's urgency to see you may be because they have been rejected by a significant other, job opportunity, or feeling down on their luck.

DATING DADDY

Over time, I learned what certain expressions Leo said meant based on the timing of his communication. A few times, I think he genuinely cared about my well-being and would follow up with me about some personal and professional issues during the day. However, much of his communication took place between sunset and sunrise. In my naïveté, I did not realize his intentions until later. I didn't realize the "hey" and "wya" texts were breaking the ice before he asked to see me. I did not realize that his "I miss you" most likely meant he missed certain parts of my anatomy and not my spirit. Whether he had other intentions was never clear due to his mysterious nature.

My friends were also puzzled about Leo's peculiar departure because it sounded like he "disappeared off the face of the earth." But that was just it. Leo's cryptic messages had become so much a part of my experience with him that I didn't realize he may have actually needed help. Behind those final "hey" and late night messages was someone who may have wanted more than a romantic rendezvous. He may have had a dire need and in my quest to let him go, I ignored him. The final "wya" may have been a cry for a place to stay for the evening. The "hey" may have been a plea for a meal. I don't know nor may I ever have the chance to find out.

You may have experienced similar pleas from people whom you have unhealthy relationships with but feel bound to, for whatever reason. They may have proven their worth to you in the past and now you feel obligated to them for something they did for you years ago. Your sense of loyalty may be wrapped around that person for dear life even though their purpose in your life has expired. It's hard to fathom that the relationship needs to be cut off or less than what it currently is, but sometimes the most loving thing you can do for them is to let them go. God can do more for that person than you can ever do. If

He leads you away from an unfruitful relationship, know that He will take care of you and is more than capable of taking care of them.

When you realize your purpose, it becomes clearer what does not align with it. Use that as motivation to make the changes needed to cut unhealthy relationships, habits, or ideals that are not aligned with your divine path in life. Those "hey," "hello," "I miss you" messages or phone calls are only distractions on your journey and every perceived need is not an emergency. You do not have to answer everyone who calls on you. Yes, be kind to others and treat others better than the way you wish to be treated. But know that God has empowered you for the journey He has for you. If He does not work through you to bless the person who reaches out to you, He will use someone else and that is perfectly fine.

> *"If He leads you away from an unfruitful relationship, know that He will take care of you and is more than capable of taking care of them."*

I felt guilty for not being available when Leo probably needed me, but it took a long time to break the soul tie of this relationship and I could not afford to look back. I could not afford sabotaging my future by remaining connected to him. My friends knew I had just ended a chapter in my life because I did one of my two rituals. Following a breakup or ending of a season in life, I either cut or color my hair or I change my phone number. After the Leo season ended, I changed my number.

BREAKING BAD BEHAVIOR

Another lesson from Leo was how establishing clear boundaries teaches others how to treat you. There is a popular saying that what you allow is what will continue. At first, you may be so captivated by a man or woman's good traits that you overlook their indiscretions. You ignore the fact that they get upset easily because they always buy you dinner or pay your phone bill. You may disregard that they're distracted by their phone or what's on the TV when you're at home alone. At least you're spending "quality" time together, right?

One way to stop the unwanted behavior is to set clear boundaries and to reinforce them. It is no good if you say to someone they cannot treat you in a certain way and not do anything about future violations. I learned this while serving as a site supervisor for an extended school program that serviced kindergarten through eighth grade students. Over a course of five years, my programs doubled in size, which meant there were more knee scrapes, more responsibilities and more behavioral issues. I've led teams of six to ten gifted and unique employees in facilitating programs that included between sixty to 130 students each day. Some of the staff knew how to manage large groups of students with minimum effort while others felt the need to get the students' attention using a louder tone and were often drained by the end of the program day.

As I observed my staff and provided on-the-spot coaching, I noticed some key things. What I realized was that the staff who felt they had to yell to get the students' attention lacked the ability to establish rules and follow through with age appropriate consequences such as time away from the activity. Conversely, the staff who relied more on nonverbal communication—such as hand clapping or competitions for the most "silent" students—established the rules at the beginning of their rotation and reinforced them if the students violated. Because the students were held accountable for their actions, they listened to the facilitator when they spoke and rarely had to be referred to me for acting out. Similarly, if you establish boundaries with your significant other and do not enforce them, they will not respect you and will continue to cross the line you've set.

Reinforcing your boundary includes acknowledging those behaviors that are in alignment with your values as well as having difficult conversations when others violate them. I was great at positive reinforcement and horribly inconsistent in discouraging bad behaviors in my relationships. I learned by trial and error with Leo more about my values in romantic relationships and how to reinforce those boundaries with consistency. I learned this lesson the hard way. If I had gotten this lesson earlier, I would not have been in relationship with him for long. Instead, we stayed connected for almost four years because I was unclear about what I wanted and sent mixed messages.

> *"Knowing your worth will help with setting boundaries that are straightforward and unambiguous."*

It was critical that I learned to reinforce my new boundaries to affect real change. I could not say I wanted to break things off one minute and run to him the next. But I did. These mixed signals also revealed my weaknesses. He learned what to do or say to get me to give in to him. When someone knows your weaknesses, they can use them as bait to reel you in. They will continue using the same bait until it does not work anymore or they do not get a reaction from you. If they realize giving you roses will ease your anger, for instance, they will shower you with flowers for every indiscretion instead of changing their behavior. Once that no longer works, they will either need to change or get creative and find the next thing that will pacify your anger or hurt.

It is absolutely key that you understand your worth. Knowing your worth will help with setting boundaries that are straightforward and unambiguous. Saying something may take energy, but it is worth the effort. Not going on that one date after someone has violated your trust may be the loss of a free meal, but you're worth more than that. Realize that not saying or doing something to reinforce your boundary is another way of giving the other person permission to mistreat you. Most important, do not go back on what you value or you risk being in an unending cycle with the person or others who come after them. Real love is when people can honor your boundaries and modify their behavior out of respect to you.

GET WISDOM, NO STRINGS ATTACHED

Finally, I learned wisdom doesn't come with age or maturity. True wisdom comes from God. I believe there is much to learn from everyone and every experience. However, when sex is involved, there is often more at play and it comes with a price. Advice may be offered with the hopes of getting one step closer to the bedroom. A listening ear may be extended to plot emotional pathways to a love making session. A shoulder to cry on may lead to a tear soaked shirt that needs to be taken off. I know that last one was a bit exaggerated and there are men and women who genuinely care for you, even if you both don't end up in the bedroom. However, it is important to keep in mind the nature of your relationship with the person when seeking a wise perspective.

Without knowing much about my father until we lived together, I believed him to be wise. I assumed his life experiences taught him to make better choices over time and that he would have some sage insight to share with me once we got close. However, most of our conversations were filled with his regrets. Regrets about career choices and financial hardships often took up our discussions. He expressed more about his personal regrets than he ever did about the lack of our relationship.

If nothing else, I guess I learned what not to do from his mistakes, right?

Leo, on the other hand, was a man of certainty. While Leo's foresight was something I cherished, it was the same thing that gave him an edge on how to draw me closer. My naïveté gave him home court advantage and the leverage to dictate the relationship for a considerable amount of time. I got caught up because I didn't have a clue what was going on. All I knew was that I was attracted to Leo, but could not identify reasons beyond the surface until this period of reflection.

It would prove to be easier to break the physical ties with Leo than to break him from my thoughts. But both were hard to do. He knew what to say to pique my interest like leaving a path of bread crumbs to catch a mouse. I was so fascinated by the tasty crumbs that I followed them to wherever Leo led me. Though the physical space of our rendezvous changed, the same tactics kept me hooked for longer than I wanted to stay. I desired what he had to offer, which was the wise perspective I longed for from my father, but I now know there were better places to have that need met.

According to Proverbs 2:6, both wisdom and understanding come from the Lord and I believe a relationship with Jesus offers us wisdom if we seek Him. This was evident in the encounter at the well. The woman knew of the Messiah and declared that He would impart His wisdom to her people (John 4:25)—which means she knew the value of Christ even though she did not know who He was or that He was right there standing before her! Even before he made known who He was, I believe Jesus met the Samaritan woman at the well with an understanding heart. He understood she was not perfect and had a history of failed relationships.

What I love is that Jesus required nothing more of her than

to seek Him to fulfill her needs. He had more to offer her than anything she could have gained from the men whom she was involved with romantically. But unlike the men, His only motive was for her to thirst no more by seeking Him.

Likewise, He can meet our deepest needs with no strings attached. The thing to keep in mind, however, is that God's ways of doing things seem counterintuitive to the way we operate. Sometimes the path will seem clear and every sign you see will point you in the direction He would have you to go. Other times, you will venture on the wrong path when you realize it was not paved by Him. If we want wisdom, we can obtain it through His written and spoken Word. Occasionally, the process of gaining wisdom is not in the good choices we make, but it is gleaned from some of our biggest mistakes.

In the end, God's unconditional love is available to us no matter where we are in our journey. This was something I was unfamiliar with while I was connected to Leo because his attention came with a cost. I believed God loved me, but I had a limited view of it. If I sinned, I believed He did not love me nor would He answer my prayers. He would not have an intimate relationship with me as long as I had sex outside of marriage. But if I was able to cut off Leo for good, I would be able to restore a right relationship with Him. This merit based love may be how we operate, but it is not how God operates. I would come to know His unconditional love on a more intimate level much later.

DEION:
Dating for Daddy Potential

Newly married, graduated, and celebrating 30 years of life at a friend's birthday party.
May 2014

CHAPTER 13

LOVE & FOOTBALL

AFTER MY EXPERIENCE WITH LEO, I didn't expect to find love for quite some time. To be honest, I wasn't even looking for it. God could have waited as long as He wanted to before He brought someone new to my life. I expected to completely detach from everything and live life freely. My plan was to remain single and to enjoy the company of positive people. Then again, Woody Allen's quote rang true for my next relationship: "If you want to make God laugh, tell him about your plans." I guess He thought I was a standup comedian because I told God I was going to be single for a long time. But as you will soon discover, things did not go as I thought they would.

CHANCE MEETING

Deion and I could have met years ago, but fate had other plans. We attended the same high school, but I didn't notice him because he was a sophomore my senior year and I was more focused on going to college than getting into a relationship. Before you judge me, he was only one year younger than me but with a fall birthday, he was two grades behind me.

Another opportunity to meet would have been through our Greek organization affiliations. After college, I knew two of his older fraternal brothers who share a July birthday with me. Each year, for two or three years, we collaborated for an annual Cancer Bash house party that was well attended.

It was not until we became "friends" on social media that

he contacted me in response to a post I made about my summer plans in March of 2010. I played in a co-ed sand volleyball league with my supervisor, a few co-workers and their spouses. On this particular post, I expressed how excited I was for our upcoming season and Deion responded that he would like to check out one of our games. It didn't seem as creepy as it could have been because he used our Greek affiliation to make the connection. I was oblivious to his advances because I had broken ties with Leo months before and I was not ready.

By August, my team had one or two games remaining in the regular season when Deion came to mind. I reached out to him on a Sunday to tell him about our game the next evening, which was held in a park in a more affluent area northeast of Indianapolis. Deion accepted the invitation and would be my first guest to attend in the four years I played with the team. What was most surprising was the moment my supervisor, and team captain, said, "Hi, Deion" when he saw him! How did my supervisor know Deion? To my amazement, Deion worked with our company that summer, but we never met until that August night!

Now that I had a guest, I played a little more competitively and I brought the heat to help our team win the game! To celebrate, Deion and I went down the street from the park and talked over ice cream. Deion mistakenly believed I liked him by the way I rubbed my leg against his, but I actually I was trying to get some of the sand off me from the volleyball game. Nonetheless, we had undeniable chemistry. If it had not been for closing time at the creamery, we would have been there talking for hours. From that night forward, we did not go a day without talking to each other.

That evening was memorable for several reasons, including the fact that Deion traveled a great distance to support a girl he didn't know. He worked over ten hours as a teacher's aide during the day and an athletic coach after school, yet he drove almost an hour out of his way to my game. Deion's love of sports may have been why he reached out to me, but sports are what repelled me from guys like him. Deion was a high school and collegiate athlete. And I never wanted to date an athlete because of their reputation as womanizers. Yet, Deion seemed different. He was more like the guy next door who just so happens to be athletic.

When we met, Deion played for a local semi-pro football team and, after the night of ice cream, I began attending his games every week. With my limited knowledge of football, I did not know much about Deion's position as a safety. Going to Deion's games was always exciting for me as I learned more about his role and just enjoyed watching him play.

After three weeks of dating, Deion made our relationship official on September 12, 2010, which was the evening before his birthday. I had taken him to dinner and we went back to my apartment to chat. During the conversation, he talked about relationships and chemistry before asking me to be his girlfriend. From there our relationship flourished as we had more intimate conversations, including the very sensitive topic: our upbringings. I felt connected to him because he was also a survivor and did not succumb to unhealthy alternative lifestyles, which we both could have.

YEAR OF FIRSTS

From there, Deion and I became known as the "fun" couple among our friends. We loved to play! We enjoyed taking chances and trying new things together. Our first Christmas as a couple was a new experience for me being in an actual relationship over the holidays. At that time, I was working through personal finance coach Dave Ramsey's Baby Step #2, which is paying off debts using the debt snowball, and I was focused on living within my means. As a result, Deion did not receive a real Christmas gift from me. I made cards with various favors he could redeem at any time such as a home-cooked meal and other things. Imagine my shock when he showered me with new boots, perfume, and other items that could only fit in the largest gift bag you can get at the store.

Wow! This is a REAL relationship with REAL gifts! You've got to do better, Shavonne.

Embarrassed by the lack of gifts my Love received at Christmas, I was determined to make up for it on Valentine's Day. Paying off my debt was still a priority, but I decided to mix creativity with investing in a proper gift for the day of love. The night included painting on two canvases that I purchased and a gift bag for Deion with some cologne I thought would smell good on him and his favorite candy. He loved Cajun food and I planned to have dinner at a local New Orleans inspired restaurant before going to a live performance featuring Chrisette, my friend.

The date was executed as planned and we returned to my apartment for the evening. Deion had done so much for me with his Christmas gifts that I didn't care he hadn't given me a gift. As I went to my room to change into my pajamas, it appeared that he was going into his gym bag to get his when he pulled out his gift for me! It was a black Nintendo Wii! I beamed!

Just a few weeks prior, we went to an electronics store to pick up some new games for his video game system and I made some comments about some of my favorite games, including Mario Brothers and other games including the next thing he pulled out of his bag—which was the MICHAEL JACKSON: THE EXPERIENCE game!!! That game alone was enough to make me melt like a groupie.

DATING DADDY

See, I love Michael Jackson! Like REALLY love Michael Jackson! I have studied his choreography and aspired to perform like him should I become famous. In the meantime, I included his dance moves in the choreography for the Praise Dance ministry, for the youth theatre camp I supervised, and in the living room when I'd dance alone. In high school, my friends and I shared a cab to our co-op experience at a local hospital and every morning we would be stopped by the longest train in America. I made it a point to jump out of the car, do the MJ skip and kick from our cab all the way to the train tracks and back, which was usually a hundred feet away, while passing several cars along the way. THAT'S how much I love MJ!

So, when Deion pulled the MJ Experience out of his bag, I fell in love! I loved that he paid attention to what I said. His gift represented his attentiveness to me and his desire to make me happy. I thought I was making headway in the gift department, but his gift definitely upstaged mine. I was too excited about MJ to pay much attention to notice the Mario game he had also gotten me. He set up the game system and we stayed up late playing the games until Deion was tired out and I was dancing solo. I'd look back between moves and see Deion's admiration as well as the proud look on his face, like the boyfriend who got a hole in one. He most certainly did.

To celebrate our first anniversary, we took a three-day cruise to Nassau, Bahamas. It was the first cruise experience for both of us, filled with wonder and tranquility. I still remember the magic of waking up to him resting peacefully with a glow from the sun shining on his chocolate complexion under the white covers. I could just stare at him for hours. It was so majestic. Though the trip was short, it was a time filled with bliss and a magnificent celebration of our first year together before returning to the reality of life.

CAREER CHANGES & CROSSFIT

And the reality was that we both got the itch to pursue new career opportunities. From childhood, Deion dreamed of becoming a firefighter. He told me about it one evening in my bathroom while I was preparing for our date. In the early days, many of our best conversations took place in the bathroom but I remember this one like it was yesterday. He described his dream with such passion and enthusiasm as I listened while straightening my hair over the sink. He asked me if I had seen the movie *Ladder 49* and other questions to gauge if I could see myself with a firefighter. All I knew was that I was happy to be with someone who possessed this level of passion about their dreams. He seemed more than ready to pursue firefighting opportunities more aggressively, but the recruitment process would prove to be especially competitive for him as a Black firefighter.

> "It was in these moments that I felt like his friend and love. It was the best of both worlds!"

Soon after this bathroom confessional, several recruiting opportunities came up and I did everything I could to support him. One of the first phases of each process included a written exam. After work, I'd go straight to Deion's apartment to cook him meals while he reviewed the study guides. When he finished studying, we'd watch one of our favorite shows or play video games for the rest of the evening until it was time to go to bed. It was in these moments that I felt like his friend and love. It was the best of both worlds! And his studying paid off as evidenced in the high scores he received on the written exams. But each recruitment process drew several hundred to a little over a thousand applicants who shared the same dream, and Deion was turned down for each one. Deion's chances may have been slim with such a large pool of applicants, but I always knew he possessed the drive and vigor to live it out.

Motivated by his discipline and physique, I sought out more effective ways of getting in shape. Long ago were the days I could eat what I wanted and remain the size of a toothpick. Now, I had to begin making healthier choices, but I did not know how. I would ask Deion for fitness advice and decided to take initiative to lose the weight I had picked up since working professionally. One day, my friend and I were walking along the Monon Trail in the Broad Ripple area of Indianapolis. During that first walk, we lucked upon a building with an open garage door where we saw a workout class taking place. The exercise looked rigorous and challenging, and I thought, *What if I joined this gym?* It wasn't long after that I joined the "cult" famously known as CrossFit.

Once I joined, the CrossFit workouts killed me—but I loved it! Immediately, I got familiar with the new lingo. For example, the workout facility was called a box. And I was such a novice to lifting weights that I made silly mistakes. For instance, the women's barbell is thirty-five pounds and I mistakenly thought I was lifting forty-five pounds after I added one ten-pound plate to each side of the bar. Unbeknownst to me, I was actually lifting fifty-five pounds. Who knew you were supposed to count the amount of weight added on both sides of the bar for the total?

What I especially came to enjoy were the Olympic Weightlifting classes offered by my box. The owner, Coach Red, was not only a regular CrossFit regional competitor, but he was training several athletes in our box to compete nationally as Olympic weightlifters. These classes proved to be a nice break from the intensity of the CrossFit classes. After each Oly workout, I'd shared my excitement with Deion, but it would take time before

I fully committed to the Olympic Weightlifting program.

Around this time, I was informed that one of my mentors in college had recently announced his retirement and this caused me to reflect on a career change as well. As a first-generation college student, I was enrolled in a student support program that provided academic support and social opportunities to retain students from similar backgrounds to mine. This particular mentor was the director of the program and I admired how his work didn't seem like work at all. Yes, he worked diligently to ensure the program had sufficient resources for the services they provided, but there were fun programs led by his office. After doing some research on the director's professional background, I realized my next step would be to earn a master's degree in education. So, while Deion continued pursing his dream of becoming a firefighter, I began considering graduate programs that would aid me in shifting toward a career in higher education.

AN UNFORGETTABLE HOLIDAY

From day one, Deion supported me in maintaining my individuality. He learned my strengths and was able to provide feedback when I considered major life decisions. When I decided to go to graduate school, for instance, Deion supported me from the moment I took the standardized test exam through the on-campus interview process with words of encouragement and support. I was accepted by both graduate programs I applied to, but they both required me to move an hour away from home. I don't know how he felt about me moving away, but Deion was supportive of my decision to further my education.

With my big move approaching in August 2012, we wanted to spend as much time together as possible. I stayed with Deion for my last two weeks of freedom and we had fun binge-watching every episode of the *Fresh Prince of Bel Air*. Ironically, the timing of the final episode when everyone moved out of the house was the same time as my move for graduate school. We experienced the same feelings of sorrow as the characters on the screen who were also transitioning from what they had known.

My graduate assistantship was as a residence hall coordinator for a small private university an hour west of home. With the demands of grad school, my assistantship, and the physical distance between us, Deion and I did our best to stay connected. We spoke on the phone every day and he spent a few weekends per month with me. I opted to take my courses in the city Deion resided in, our hometown, and would make time to see him before returning to my assistantship in residence life in the other city. Still, the visits felt short because of the demands of graduate school.

A few months later, my first Thanksgiving in grad school became one I will never forget. Deion asked if we could have dinner with his family. At first, I was a little saddened that I would not see my mom, sis, and her seven-month-old daughter, but I remembered he had sacrificed the past few holidays to be with my family. So I spent Thanksgiving eve with my family to assist with the meal prep and then drove to his apartment on an empty stomach where I prepared for his family's gathering.

By the time we made it to the venue of his family's dinner, I was starving! Mission one was to find the food table and eat. Once we entered the banquet hall, I was welcomed by members of his family, including his lovely grandmother! She was the only face I was familiar with and was also the only family member who knew Deion's secret.

The food fulfilled me so much so that I cleared my plate and went back for more. Toward the end of dinner, I was in such a state of contentment that I didn't think it was odd for one of

Deion's closest friends to show up. As I was chatting with this friend, Deion's aunt asked if anyone had anything to share. That is when Deion stepped forward with as much passion as a music video from the R&B group Boyz II Men and said, "I'm thankful for my family and my girlfriend who I don't want to be my girlfriend anymore..."

I was completely oblivious to what he was trying to say, but he had my full attention now. He continued, "I want her to be my fiancé." Now, I was in total, complete shock! My jaw dropped. My eyes widened to the point of almost popping out of the sockets. I could not move. I didn't move until Deion realized I was stuck stiff and he waved me toward him for his romantic proposal on bended knee. Of course, I said yes!

A long time ago, I remember the pastor of the church "where Jesus is exalted and the Word is explained" saying that you'll know a potential mate is the one when you can "see" no one else. It's as if you have tunnel vision and you won't desire other people outside of your relationship. Deion was that and more to me. When I met him, I did not have eyes for any other man. I would find out years later that other men had made advances while I was with him, but my focus was locked and loyalty devoted. So when he got down on one knee in front of his family, I was absolutely sure this was the guy I would spend the rest of my life with. No challenge big or small could change that for me.

After I said yes, I realized he also invited my best friend Chrisette who had been hiding in the room during the proposal. As soon as I saw her, I screamed. Immediately, I asked her to be my maid of honor and she gladly accepted.

In both of our inner circles, we were known as a fun and active couple. We enjoyed spending time together listening to music, playing videogames, going to the movies, working out, and simply being on the go. My friends and sorority sisters would say that he got my quirkiness because he was also quirky. I don't agree about the part where I'm quirky, but Deion understood me in a way no other man could. He was the man who could switch from a suit to sweats seamlessly! We had fun together and I could see us in the places I wanted to go in life. It would seem this was a match made in heaven, but there was a storm brewing over the horizon.

CHAPTER 14

GONE AWOL

IN THE MILITARY, THERE IS a term called AWOL, which means Absent With Out Leave. It is when a soldier on assignment leaves their post on their own inclination. They desert their responsibilities, especially when they are at odds with their circumstances. I was always told that men are careful whom they choose to marry and they do not take that commitment lightly. So when they choose to marry a woman, they plan to be married for life. Then how did such a sweet romance manifest into my husband's abrupt departure? What were the events that led up to Deion going AWOL from our marriage? I'll pick up the story from Thanksgiving 2012 after he proposed…

EMERGING SHARDS

I returned to school excited about my recent engagement and made plans to spend my second year of grad school closer to him. I prayed one of those famous promise prayers: "God, if you help me, I'll do more of (fill in the blank of your spiritual shortcoming) for You!" My prayer was that God would grant me an opportunity in Indianapolis and I promised Him I would go to church EVERY Sunday!

Well, you have to be ready to follow through with a promise you give to God! After months of searching, I obtained a new position in Indianapolis and now I had to make good on my promise. By June 2013, I had moved in with Deion and his hospitality made me feel welcome, but soon after, I received a text from Leo…

"Hey"

I did not respond.

By July, Deion and I found our stride, but this was also the point where he started to withdraw from me. I thought it was a normal part of a relationship, but something within me would not settle. I thought I was being paranoid when it was actually my intuition prompting me of something I feared most. A few days after my birthday in mid-July, I became aware that Deion was involved with two other women. All feelings of being "in love" escaped my body instantly and I experienced an excruciating hurt I had never felt before. It was like having the life sucked out of me, leaving a bewildered girl who was unsure of her present—let alone her future—with the man I thought I once loved. Part of me was ready to call off the wedding altogether but I was advised not to rush the decision by a close friend. Plus, this was the guy I thought I was supposed to spend forever with!

How could we move forward? Could I ever trust him again?

So many questions spun through my mind and in the midst of the confusion, I received a text…

"Hey"

This time I responded and told Leo what all had happened. He listened as I went back and forth in my decision to stay or leave my relationship with Deion. Leo recommended I find solace in God's word and to stick it out with Deion. He believed things could change. Though I could not fully trust Leo because of our history, I took his word for it.

A few days later, Deion and I decided to stay together and talked about the changes we needed from each other to make our relationship work. He committed to going to church with me every Sunday and, at least once a week, we incorporated devotionals into our time together. But like any commitments made under pressure, this change was temporary and ended before our wedding eight months later.

While on the road to repairing the trust lost in our relationship, our already fragile relationship took another hit when Deion received yet another rejection letter from a fire department. By now, this was his sixth or seventh attempt since we'd been together and he received the letter on the eve of his friend's bachelor party. He immediately broke down in a way I had not seen him do. The strong man whom I loved had been reduced to tears after reading the first line of the letter. It was as if I was witnessing the answer to the opening line of the poem *Harlem* by Langston Hughes: "What happens to a dream deferred?" Cowered down before me, I saw what happens. I witnessed my future husband experiencing the heaviness and brokenness of his lifelong dream deferred.

He wanted to stay at home but I wouldn't let him. Nothing I could say would have eased the brunt of the news. Almost immediately, I called his best friend Damion, who was also the best man, and asked him to come over. Damion was at the door within moments and they talked until finally we convinced him to go to the bachelor party.

Initially, I told my fiancé to go the bachelor party to lift his spirits, but he came back with news I did not expect to hear.

"I'm joining the military!"

What? Why? Hold up! How did going to a bachelor party motivate you to join the military?

He explained that he couldn't start a family without a solid career. He wanted to ensure me and our future children would be taken care of. I respected his reasoning but I had already experienced being the significant other of a military man with Cliff. Though it was brief, the military created a distance between us and changed Cliff. Now the man I was planning to marry was going down a similar path?

DISTANCE MAKES THE HEART GROW FONDER

After going back and forth with various branches, Deion committed to serving in the National Guard, but you would never guess what his military occupational specialty, or MOS, was; it was as a 12M—a firefighter. Obviously, this was an opportunity for him to live out his dream even if he was not a civilian firefighter. However, his military training would commence at the end of April 2014 and go for twenty-four weeks, which caused us to move up our original wedding date from June to March to ensure we would be married before he left.

On Friday, March 14, 2014, we were married at a country club in the presence of our family, friends, and members of our fraternity and sorority. Our wedding colors were a Malibu blue and tangerine orange. On the day of our windy wedding ceremony, I was oddly calm, according to the people who were around me before the wedding. Was every bride supposed to be a frantic mess on their wedding day? I missed that memo. Besides a couple of hiccups, the day went without a hitch and we enjoyed the reception (and specialty cupcake centerpieces).

The next day, we took a short honeymoon to an all-inclusive resort in Jamaica. It was relaxing and what I enjoyed most was our quest for jerk chicken on the beach each day during the lunch hour. We also went on a tubing excursion off the resort in water that was so clear, clean, and refreshing. The heaviness of our fate in the coming month was far from my mind.

Love stricken, we returned home and cancelled all commitments that week. We spent much of our last month together in each other's embrace, soaking up every moment we could.

Neither of us wanted the other to see us crying as his

departure neared. The Sunday before, we went to the playoff game between the Pacers and the Hawks. It was a great game and it allowed me to get out some of my sadness through the adrenaline rush of the game, but on the way home it happened—tears poured from my eyes, making it hard to see the road. Deion tried to console me at stoplights, but the dams of my eyelids failed to hold back the tears from pouring forth as I thought about our six months apart.

That Wednesday morning was the big day. I was to drive him to the spot where he would be transported to basic training. I left the house in one of his Army shirts that was at least two sizes too big for me and, on the drive, he tried to fight his tears but he could not resist. I could only imagine what was going through his mind as he prepared for his new journey alone. His eyes were bloodshot red and when we hugged, I held on as tightly as a toddler does with their teddy. With that last kiss, I watched him walk into the building and then drove off to campus to prepare for my group's final presentation in our capstone class.

A week later I received my first call from Deion at check-in. It was days before the commencement ceremony for my graduate degree. Though his words sounded scripted, his voice was never sweeter to my ears. To honor him, I brought one of his extra Army caps on stage when my name was called and saluted him in tears as I received my diploma. It was as much his degree as it was mine due to the sacrifices he made to support me while in graduate school.

Now I had to find a job.

I needed something to occupy my mind and to distract me from my sadness and deep longing for the man I loved with all my being. Every day after I graduated, I put in eight hours per day to update my résumé, apply to numerous positions, prepare for interviews, interview over the phone, interview on campuses, and complete second-round interviews, but nothing stuck. I could not secure a job for the life of me!

But even while Deion was bound in unfamiliar territory away from family and friends, he encouraged me despite his own fears and struggles. He prayed for me and encouraged me even while he was living outside of his comfort zone. I missed him terribly and his encouragement during this time showed me that he was truly the rock of our family and could be a leader at home.

IRREPARABLE DAMAGES

When Deion returned in November, we struggled. He returned home without a civilian job and dealt with his issues by internalizing everything. Meanwhile, I began working a part-time job at the local community college and babysat for a friend three to four nights each week. In December, I picked up some contract work as a coordinator for a mentoring program and Deion found a seasonal job that made him miserable. I didn't mind working to support our family because he had sacrificed for me just months before so I encouraged him to quit his job.

In early spring, I was offered a full-time job an hour away from home; at the same time a local fire department announced its upcoming recruitment process. Deion applied and successfully moved beyond the steps he didn't pass the first time that he'd applied to this same fire department. This time he made it all the way to the near-final round but was dismissed and was in the last hundred or so candidates remaining of the 1,200 applicants—another painful blow sending him further into himself.

At home, I felt like he had checked out and that I was in the marriage alone. In my desperation, I turned to the devotionals in Stormie Omartian's book, *Power of a Praying Wife*. After a while, I noticed some improvements in my husband and took this as evidence that the prayers and devotionals worked. For instance, I focused on praying for his career and he obtained a full-time position soon after. With the new job, our intimacy increased and we enjoyed simple tasks together again. Yet there was still something missing.

That's when I took my faith a step further and returned to what I knew—church. In late spring of 2015, I began visiting the church I currently attend. I snuck to services as if I was having an affair with God because I primarily attended when my husband was away for the weekend, which was starting to increase in frequency. He spent more time with an unmarried male friend on business and personal trips out of the country while I was left behind. After a while, my focus shifted from praying for my marriage to working on my development in hopes that a change in me would improve the marriage. Every Sunday, I felt that God ministered directly to me. Unable to change what was going on at home, I could find the answers for my life at church, but my marriage was nearing a crossroad.

We were emotionally disconnected and did not know how to turn things around. We were not having in-depth conversations anymore. Deion was distant physically and emotionally.

He must not be attracted to me.

I kicked up my efforts to take care of my temple and to be the epitome of a "good wife." Even after an exhausting day at work, I made time to work out and to cook before crashing for the night, only to wake up five hours later to do it again. I dressed in more revealing clothes on dates without as much as a glance from him. Despite all my efforts, his distance grew more and more palpable until we barely made love anymore. Nothing I did could break whatever funk was going on within him.

By August 2015, I was at my lowest point of exhaustion. I was tired of my efforts going unnoticed in what seemed like a marriage of one. When Deion accompanied his friend on his annual two-week business trip to China in late July, I prayed in despair for our marriage. I cried to God, *Our marriage cannot continue like this!* Soon after my attention was drawn away by a simple text message in the midst of my desperation.

"Hey"

Why did Leo ALWAYS seem to contact me when my relationship with Deion was fragile? He had texted me right after I found out Deion was unfaithful, and now he was contacting me when I felt unloved in my marriage and Deion was out of town. In the past, I minimized his advances because I was secure in my relationship, but this time, I did not delete it or ignore it. Leo's text came during Deion's second week in China. As I read it, I thought about the five years I had gone without being physical with anyone else but Deion. After months of sowing my all into the relationship there was no return and I felt empty. I had done all I could to support Deion and our marriage, but he stopped investing into me. Into us. And I did what I never thought I would do. I returned to what was familiar and connected with Leo. And afterwards, my regret was not that I was unfaithful, but it was that I was unfaithful with Leo.

"And I did what I never thought I would do."

As a side note, I truly believe men can sense when there is trouble in a relationship paradise. Or maybe my guard was down because I received more male attention during the months leading to my rendezvous with Leo and I entertained it. Where I once ignored all other guys who tried to hit on me, even with a wedding band on, I now started to turn around with a smile when I heard a compliment. When former guys who had my number sent inappropriate messages, I no longer ignored them or blocked their numbers. I was enjoying all the attention that I had not received in the absence of Deion's affection.

It was during this time I believe he caught on that something changed with me. He asked if someone else had my attention, which I admitted to in a roundabout way, but I did not divulge much more. With Deion's growing suspicion, I began catching him looking through my phone when I was not in the room. What soon followed were conversations about the state of our marriage. After months of me initiating these conversations, the tables had turned and he was now making them a priority. In an effort to restore my marriage, I reestablished my boundaries with other men cold-turkey. Unfortunately, it may have been too late.

BEGINNING OF THE END

Just five years before on September 12th, 2010, I had taken my husband out for a pre-birthday dinner and by the end of the evening he asked me to be his lady. This year was different. Having been married for almost a year and a half, we had grown distant and I wanted to reignite the spark. Deion's birthday fell on his weekend to train at the military base an hour south of where we lived. I wanted him to enjoy his birthday and took him for an intimate pre-birthday dinner at Rick's Boatyard Cafe, a popular restaurant situated on a small lake with a great view and beautiful sunsets. On his actual birthday, September 13th, I had a surprise HandleBar outing planned with his close friends. It took a lot of effort and energy to plan this surprise and it all came together the day before. But we almost did not make it to the HandleBar.

Following the pre-birthday dinner on Saturday evening, my husband reluctantly took pictures with me. I thought his hesitation was because he never really liked to take pictures to begin with, but later realized there was more to it. Once we returned home and I looked at the photos, I noticed something different in his face. It was as if he was being forced to be there. Forced to be with me. Feeling rejected, I decided to ask him how he felt about us. He replied that he didn't want to get into it because he didn't want to spoil his birthday. In the back of my mind, I knew it would be awkward if we didn't address this tonight before the big surprise with his friends so I persisted. I thought we could address whatever was bothering him to clear the air that evening and he would be able to enjoy his surprise the next day. What he shared totally shook me.

"Our relationship has run its course," he said.

How does a marriage run its course if it is supposed to last a lifetime???

In so many words, he said he no longer loved me and that he wanted a divorce. He said he wrestled with the decision since the beginning of the year, which meant he had thought about this for at least nine months. *No wonder I felt distance.* I knew our relationship was distant but I didn't believe in divorce. I never expected it to be easy, but you're supposed to ride it out, right? I fell all the way apart. On one hand, I have wanted Deion to have everything he wanted in life, but I wanted him to have that with me. Now, I was faced with him choosing to seek what he desired without me. That night I wrestled with the decision to separate or to divorce, but he had already made up his mind.

His birthday was an emotionally draining day, to say the least. With little to no sleep, Deion reported to base for his military obligations that morning. Meanwhile I was at home wanting to reach out to someone but did not know what to do or who to call. So I called my mother and she answered in tears saying, "I don't want to die!"

Huh?

I could not make this up! Those were her exact words as soon as she answered the phone. She had checked herself into the hospital after she had reached yet another low. She explained that a few months earlier she had relapsed and it had spiraled out of control. In this moment, her oldest baby needed her so badly, but I couldn't let her know about my marriage under these circumstances. I've maintained an independent relationship with my mom for as long as I had known but I really needed her. I needed her more than ever and she couldn't be there for me. I listened to her and spent the rest of the day slowly preparing for Deion's return from base.

Deion returned home early that afternoon and we went through the motions as I drove him to the surprise HandleBar. We celebrated his birthday and most of his friends who were present had no clue this would be the last time they would see us together. It was like any other birthday the past five years, filled with fun and Deion's silly behavior. That evening I drove us home. Both of us were inebriated and he immediately passed out.

CHAPTER 15

LOVING ON EGGSHELLS

BEFORE MY LIFE-CHANGING SPIRITUAL journey took off, there were some damaging behaviors I was not aware of in my relationship with Deion. I had made him my idol. And by making Deion the top priority in my life, this had a negative impact on the most important relationship of my life—with God. Instead of living out my faith, I took the passive route and walked on eggshells to please the man I married. I did the same thing with emotional matters. I avoided saying things I thought would upset him and was dishonest about my feelings to avoid him rejecting my truth. I learned that trying to love Deion on eggshells, by hiding concerns of faith and my heart, stemmed from coping responses learned in my childhood.

> *"By making Deion the top priority in my life, this had a negative impact on the most important relationship of my life—with God."*

BLURRED LINES

Fathers teach their children lessons about love that will have a lasting effect through adulthood. These lessons are conveyed early by how they treat the mother and other women as well as through critical conversations with his daughter about love and life. Sometimes these conversations are difficult or downright uncomfortable for a father to have with his blossoming daughter but they are nonetheless critical. Psychoanalyst Joyce McFadden notes the tone that fathers set "can either negatively complicate how she believes she deserves to be treated by the opposite sex, or it can ground her in her right to be treated respectfully." In other words, daughters learn how to operate in romantic relationships from the model set forth by Dad. But what happens when the father is absent from the home? Who is left to teach her about life and love? In my case, the majority of my understanding about life came from my mother.

My relationship with Mom'ela had a significant impact on my relationship with Deion. It was not that she had a voice in our relationship or was overbearing, because I did not give her the space to do this. Like anyone who loves you, my mom was skeptical of the men I chose to date because she didn't want to see me hurt. As such, I set boundaries when it appeared that my mother would do or say something that would possibly offend Deion. This stemmed from our first Christmas together when Deion brought me all those wonderful gifts. In the middle of the family gathering, Mom'ela sarcastically threatened Deion against hurting me. Our relationship was still new and her comment changed the mood in the room and I felt I needed to protect him from her. But the need to protect the emotional needs of the people I love was a lesson learned from my relationship with my mother.

As a single mother, Mom'ela used my sister and me to meet her emotional needs. In psychology, this is known as "parentification." According to Counseling Psychologist Lisa Hooper, in emotional parentification, the child "attempts to fill an emotional or psychological void in the family for the parent and sometimes for the siblings—often becoming the parent's confidant and sole support." As previously mentioned, my mother felt like the "black sheep" of her maternal family and sought love and acceptance through her children. This meant that my sister and I were both her children and confidants simultaneously. We were her sounding boards when Mom'ela felt someone mistreated her or left her out of a family function. After hearing so many incidents where Mom'ela felt left out, I came to see her as a victim that needed my unending support. At some point, however, I started to understand the perspective of whomever she said was against her and felt guilty for agreeing with them in some matters.

Mom'ela made high emotional demands of my sister and me, which meant our emotional needs were always overlooked. One prime example was the moment when I reached out for my mother's comfort before Deion and I separated. Without so much as a hello, Mom answered the phone with a heart stopping, "I don't want to die!" No "Hi" or "Hey, Baby Girl." I was given an earful of a tearful mother who was emotionally desperate. How could I possibly tell her I was going through anything when her emotional needs superseded my own? Our emotional conversation took place while we were both in a psyche ward—she was in a physical one and I was in a mental one at home. Over the years, she complained that I didn't open up to her but I never felt I could. Her emotional needs have and seem to always supersede my own. As a result of this pattern, I learned to open up to my closest friends, and even then I didn't tell full truths out of fear of overwhelming them with the complexity of my story.

In relation to my mother, the lines between mother and child were often blurred. And the more I think about it, I wonder about her relationship with her own mother. Did Mom'ela and her siblings meet similar needs of GMa? GMa had a tendency of pushing her children away when they did not meet her needs. Likewise, my mother has the tendency of pushing my sister and me away when her emotional or other needs were not being fulfilled. It is as if she's saying, "You're not doing this for me, goodbye"—sometimes to the point of hanging up the phone when she was done unloading her cares on us. Not only has this created a distance between her and me, but I was also selective about when I showed up or was available to my mother.

HIS MOTHER OR HIS LOVER

Parentification did not only impact me in childhood, but its effects carried over into my adulthood. Because I learned to disregard my feelings, I also learned to minimize them in relationships with all who wanted to get close to me. I continued to sacrifice my needs to ensure that others had theirs met. Psychologists Marolyn Wells, Cheryl Glickauf-Hughes, and Rebecca Jones made the connection between parentification and the tendency to be hyper-vigilant to the needs of others. They noted that people who have the tendency to revere the needs of their significant others to this extent "are likely to come from families in which they were parentified, and they may continue to demonstrate parentified behaviors in their current relationships." This was true of my experience. Because I acted as a "parent" in my relationship with my mother, I also served in a "parental" role in my relationship with Deion.

It was not until the threat of him leaving that I became painfully aware of how preoccupied I was by Deion and how unhealthy that was for our relationship. It affected how I treated and communicated with him, which manifested in a need to protect his "best" interests. In the article "The Relation between Parentification and Dating Communication: The Role of Romantic Attachment-related Cognitions," Amber Madden states that parentification undermines one's ability to communicate effectively in romance. In the moments when I thought Deion needed encouragement, for instance, I tried to offer verbal motivation to help him. Later, he would say that my attempt at motivating him often served the opposite effect. It made him feel like I was trying to mother him instead of being a supportive partner. What I thought he needed to hear often emasculated him more than empowered him. Wow!

Not only did it affect how I spoke with him, but it also impacted how I treated him. I went above and beyond to ensure he had the space to do what he wanted to do, mainly leisure activities and entertainment, even if it cost me sleep and time away from him. Because I believed he was depressed when he returned from the six months of military training, I minimized my need to spend time with him when he was excited to accompany his friend on his business trips. It was a hard pill to swallow, but I learned that I was in a codependent relationship and I enabled Deion. Author R. Skip Johnson describes the enabler as the one who carries the weight of another person in a self-sacrificing manner. According to Johnson, this can take place whether the other person is able or unable to take care of themselves. This creates a scenario where the relationship is extremely one-sided. What was most striking about Johnson's claims was that even if the enabler is self-reliant, like I believed I was, their codependent behavior "is a way to mitigate fears of abandonment." In a way, codependency can be used as a faulty tactic for securing a relationship that was imbalanced anyway.

> *"I can now see how I let Deion's feelings and needs supersede my own and how it was rooted in my need for his approval and my fear of being abandoned."*

I can now see how I let Deion's feelings and needs supersede my own and how it was rooted in my need for his approval and my fear of being abandoned. In the thick of it, however, I believed I was doing it all in the name of being "supportive." One of the first things he told me early on that I held onto was that he valued the support of others. His friends from high school were his family because they were very much a part of his journey and supported him. Deion lost his father in the eighth grade and he had an estranged or nonexistent relationship with his mother. Like me, he had overcome many arduous obstacles to become successful and I admired that in him. I could see so much of myself in him that I dreamed of us being the epitome of a power couple. Each success, every medal earned or accolade accumulated along the way would have even more of a significant meaning in our years together. I dreamed big things for us even if he could not see it.

As such, I put every effort I had toward being supportive of Deion. When he played intramural sports, for instance, I was often the only girlfriend in attendance. When the significant others came to the games, I was known as the "president" of our own little girlfriends and wives club. Also, I traveled with him when he pursued firefighting recruitment processes in other cities and states. I wanted him to be able to think back on his efforts and to know without a shadow of a doubt that I was in his corner. Don't get me wrong—Deion supported my dreams too, but my mindset was such that my dreams or interests were minimized if they conflicted with his. I put them on the backburner.

BODY CONSCIOUSNESS & SELF-LOATHING

Even though I accepted some harsh realities about my role in the relationship, I struggled with Johnson's claim that an enabler's behavior can be a way to lessen the gravity of abandonment in relationships. I thought I was enough until I remembered my motivations for making drastic self-improvements. Following our engagement dinner in January 2013, I noticed his once tunnel vision and focus on me turned into a wandering eye. But I would placate myself by telling myself that I was the woman he proposed to and wanted to spend the rest of his life with. It didn't bother me until I felt I was now competing for his attention. In a study on the effects of the portrayal of African American women in hip hop culture, psychologists Dionne Stephens and April Few state, "To remain competitive in the dating market, women must try to meet men's standards of beauty." But wasn't I off the market? Why did I feel I had to compete against other women to keep my fiancé's attention?

When we talked about his infidelity at home later that summer, I soon learned he was no longer attracted to me. He said I had gained weight and the way I dressed was too conservative. He wanted me to dress in a way that showed off my assets. Ouch! His words stung because it wasn't the first time I had been judged by a man based on my visual appearance. Until Deion, I've only heard compliments about my appearance from my dad, GPa, and other men I came across. Though GMa had schooled me on this years ago, this was the first time I heard it from a man straight to my face. Nonetheless, I did not fight his argument, but I regret not saying more. Instead of holding him accountable for choosing to find "satisfaction" outside of our relationship and for his comments about my weight, I internalized his feedback about me and made it a point to be the woman he desired. I must have thought little of myself to overlook the fact that he never accepted responsibility or truly apologized for treating me in this disrespectful way. It was as if he justified his unfaithfulness because I violated some unknown standard he had in the back of his mind. Following that conversation, I went into overdrive to become the woman I thought he wanted me to be.

It was like I transformed from one extreme to the other. I went from aspiring to be classy and sophisticated like Dr. Maya Angelou, Oprah, India Arie, Lauryn Hill, and my GMa to seeking immediate methods of losing weight to be sexy for my future hubby. I was already doing CrossFit but I took it to the next level. I ate a low-calorie diet and considered waist trainers to regain and keep Deion's attention. Where I used to wear clothes that didn't reveal too much of my figure, my dresses and shorts got shorter and more revealing. In three months, I lost twenty pounds from counting calories and started getting more obvious stares from other men when Deion and I were in public. After the initial weight loss, I resolved to stick with lifestyle changes so I could maintain long-term weight loss.

I chose to forgive him. I chose to marry him. Yet, what that experience taught me, in my mind, was sex equals attraction. If we were having a healthy sex life, that means he was attracted to me. If we were going through a drought, he was not. The sting of his words replayed in my mind from the day we decided to stay together.

A DEVASTATING BREAKTHROUGH

Thou shalt have no other gods before me.
~Exodus 20:3

Parentification, codependency, or whatever other name you have for an imbalanced relationship, is a form of idol worship. An idol is any person or thing that we put higher than God. I idolized my mother. I put her needs above my own and was not vocal about my concerns. To this day, I am paralyzed by most interactions with her because I expect her to dump all her cares on me as she has in the past. In a similar way, I idolized Deion. He was the idol of my affection and there wasn't much I wouldn't do for him. I sought to protect him and his dreams at the cost of my own. But guess what? We were not built to save our family, friends, or lovers. God is.

To worship or revere people or things over God violates the

first commandment in the Bible. In Exodus 20:3, God told the children of Egypt, "Thou shalt have no other gods before me." Though this commandment was made centuries ago, I believe it is still true today. I believe God blesses us with people and things, but He wants us to put them in proper perspective. We are to keep Him as our first priority—the focus of our affection—and our other healthy values follow accordingly such as family, friends, career, etc. Ultimately, we have the choice to prioritize however we'd like, but for those of us who claim we love God, we must make the choice to put Him on the throne of our hearts. People will not be consistent. Things will break. Money will disappear, but God is eternal. When we do not make God our center, we will experience extreme heartache from choosing to ignore His wisdom in love, life, and other choices we face. He is the only One truly worthy of our endless affection.

Earlier, I made the criteria for a husband to be a man who could lead our family spiritually and there were signs Deion would not be able to do this. But I ignored them. The possibility that our marriage was coming to an end caused excruciating pain! I felt blindsided the eve of his birthday when he said he wanted out. I believed the months leading up to his birthday were just a rough patch in our marriage that we would work through. I wasn't sure why he wanted to leave. When he returned from China, we had several conversations about our distance in the marriage but I did not think it was coming to an end. All I knew was that this was the most open he had been in months and I saw it as progress, not closure. Immediately, I focused on saving my marriage instead of seeking contentment outside of it.

But he didn't. The man who asked me to be his wife and the first man I loved on this level was about to go AWOL. What would I have left? I held him in such high regard, even putting my spiritual growth on the back burner. When we met, I sung in a community gospel choir. As Deion and I got closer, my involvement in ministry and attendance in church diminished. Not because he told me not to, but because we did not connect over Christ. The foundation of our relationship centered on his interests and values more than a mutual sharing of our beliefs collectively. As a Christian, I believed the man is the head of the household and I chose to submit to him. But some of his actions and lack of motivation conflicted with my beliefs. As a result, I walked on eggshells in our marriage to avoid conflict and to be the docile wife I thought I was supposed to be.

The risk of losing Deion would come to disrupt unhealthy behaviors within me that spanned the course of my life. It would reveal the damage caused by my self-sacrificing relationship with my mother. It made clear my pattern of putting the needs of others above my own no matter the sacrifice. Even when I thought I had good self-esteem before meeting Deion, I compromised my faith to serve the needs of my man. Nothing will keep a man (or woman, fellas) if your priorities are out of whack. Period.

CHAPTER 16

UNRAVELING A FORTUITOUS MARRIAGE

*If married couples don't intentionally
choose to keep growing together,
they tacitly agree to grow apart.*
~Gary Thomas, Minister

YOU MUST BE DELIBERATE TO make a marriage work. A great marriage will not happen by chance. It takes two people who are willing to stick to each other despite all that comes against the marriage. And despite all that comes against the two individuals within it. Unfortunately, you're not only fighting new battles to remain strong. You're also fighting preconceived notions, outsiders' opinions, and old behaviors that attempt to permeate the relationship. If these go unnoticed or unaddressed, they can silently kill the union. I believe with all my heart that Deion is a good man, but there were particular elements that did not foster growth of our marriage.

LACK OF RECIPROCITY

Codependency is often associated with the behavior of those who support or enable another's alcohol or other addiction. This reminded me of the times my sister and I attended the recovery meetings with my mom. We've accompanied my mother to Narcotics Anonymous, Cocaine Anonymous, and Alcoholics Anonymous meetings and became familiar with each group's version of the Twelve Step program. Out of the twelve steps that are used in every anonymous group, there was one step that stands out most—the first step.

The first step in any anonymous group program is to admit there is a problem and that you are unable to manage what you have grown accustomed to doing. Many who drink alcohol daily may believe they're only social drinkers. It is not until tragedy hits home that many recovering alcoholics sober up and acknowledge the problem with their behavior. It could be when the alcoholic's significant other gets tired of the abusive relationship and follows through with her endless threats to uproot the children and move out. The revelation could come from something else such as the alcoholic being sick and tired of waking up with hangovers constantly. There are many sobering incidents that precede the alcoholic's awareness of her damaging behavior. And it is in the metal folding chair circles of the recovery meetings that the alcoholic comes face to face with her addictions while learning new ways to overcome addiction.

For me, it took a while to admit I was an enabler and that I operated in codependent relationships. It was not until I was faced with losing my marriage that I saw how much I invested in Deion while sabotaging myself. And it was not until I wrote this book that I realized the earlier experiences my codependency was rooted in.

Shockingly, I would learn another thing about my codependency before this book went to print. But in my story, the circle of people in my recovery room of codependency were the early readers and they reflected something back to me that was unexpected. I thought I had reached the point of admitting I had a problem and that I was well on my way to improving my life. But it was these same readers who saw clearly the connection between Leo and Deion. One person, in particular, suggested I combine the stories of Leo and Deion because the common theme between the two men was a need to set clear boundaries.

I wrestled with this. I believed they were two different men with different lessons to learn. Clearly, I was young and naïve when Leo was a part of my life. I thought my biggest lesson was that when it's time to break an unhealthy pattern, there were certain things you must do. Then obviously, with Deion I learned to not only be interested in the man I love, but to also be interested in myself. They were two different men with two unique stories, right?

Right?

But the more I thought about it the more I came to know that each of those relationships required setting expectations for how I deserved to be treated. In both relationships, I surrendered myself to the interests and convenience of the men I wanted to be with. Both relationships, especially in the end, lacked reciprocity. They were one-sided. And there was only one person who benefited in the relationship and it was not me. If I did not correct this behavior, this would continue to be the story of my life in any relationship I enter from this moment forward.

Similarly, you must be aware and acknowledge any codependent tendencies if you want to move forward and heal. Do you continually find yourself prioritizing the needs of others over your own? How many times have you made professional plans, only to cancel them when your significant other or friend says they need you (but they ALWAYS need you)? When was the last time you kept your personal appointments to take care of your nails, soak in the tub, or even deep condition your hair without bending for another? You may believe your constant sacrifices are done in the name of love for others, but you are actually acting out of self-hate. If you do not acknowledge the self-sabotaging patterns in your relationship with others, you will continue the cycle into any new relationship you enter.

Instead, it is important to seek reciprocity in your relationship with others. And let me make this absolutely clear: *You are not responsible for others' choices, consequences, or emotions.* You are not. It is important to make your needs a priority. If your significant other, family member, or others cannot respect your acts of self-care and personal boundaries, that is their issue. Again, I am not condoning irresponsible behavior. Obviously, self-care for a single person is different from someone who is married or even someone who is married with children. But demonstrating love for yourself will attract more love toward you while blocking unloving things, experiences, and people from your life. After all, isn't that what you want and deserve? Real love.

> *"You are not responsible for others' choices, consequences, or emotions."*

DISABLE THE THIRD WHEEL

Another lesson is that you must be selective of your support group for the marriage to thrive. In the beginning, it may feel like you can talk to your spouse about anything; that's part of the reason you chose to marry them. But sometimes you may want to confide in someone you trust when times are tough in your relationship. It is during those times that you must discern if the person you want to lean on is for you or for your marriage—ideally both.

If you're a Christian, you most likely heard that a marriage includes three: the husband, wife, and God. You've also read that when a couple marries, they cleave to each other to become one. Part of the couple coming together includes cutting or reducing the influence of outsiders' opinions as you form a new life with your spouse. As a couple, you must seek God together to learn how to demonstrate an everlasting love, and the Bible includes plenty of keys for doing so. Also important is to seek the counsel of a mentor couple whom both the husband and wife can turn to and be held accountable to—marriages where the men can hold the new husband accountable and the women can offer counsel to the new wife.

We did not have a mentor couple for our marriage. Instead, we both had people we confided in privately regarding the issues that were difficult to solve on our own. There were people in both of our circles who were solely for us as individuals—people who were familiar with our past relationships that didn't work, people who made a pledge to be around no matter how many relationships we go through. Ultimately, they carried the flag of Team Deion or Team Shavonne with great pride and solidarity.

In relationships including marriage, you must establish boundaries with your team and value your significant other over the individual teams. If this goes unchecked, your friends and family can become the third wheel to your relationship. How many of you have had that third wheel accompany you on a date and almost keep you from getting close to your romantic interest? They made the date awkward, right? Well, it's the same thing in marriage. If you allow someone else along for the ride in your marriage, they may keep you from establishing a deeper connection with your partner.

Instead, you must keep God and your core principles at the root of your relationship. Wise counsel will redirect you toward your partner, whereas those who are for only you may turn your attention elsewhere. You may seek counsel from genuinely happy couples who've been married longer than you, but the totality of your marriage is a process of two becoming one. It's about you two determining your relationship for yourselves. And when you keep your core values of the relationship side by side, it is as if your two wheels (or wills) are connected by a firm axle—leaving no room for a third.

Unfortunately, Deion and I did not have that. He confided in people who were never married, unhappily married or who appeared to be happier after a divorce. Though I had people who were for me, I did not discuss the issues in my marriage with Team Shavonne. I confided in women who had twenty or more years in their marriage because they appeared to be in thriving relationships. Each of them gave me the same advice, which meant that it worked for their marriages. But, you cannot expect a successful relationship when you and your partner are not operating from the same rulebook. Period.

GOING TO BATTLE...IN CHUCKS?

Finally, you need to know the type of battle you're fighting within your marriage or relationship. You wouldn't go to war in Chuck Taylors, would you? Yes, the chucks are stylish but they wouldn't provide the same security as combat boots. Combat boots are durable in swampy areas and provide stability through their sturdy grip, whereas, Chucks would most likely soak up the elements and would not be as secure on uneven pavement. Okay, Shavonne, why are we talking about shoes? I'm glad you asked! Sometimes, we try to fight our issues in life with the wrong perspective while using the wrong tools.

Unfortunately, when there was a lack of physical intimacy in my marriage I adopted the belief that Deion did not love me. I failed to realize he was in the midst of something that had absolutely nothing to do with me. He was dealing with things that only other men could identify and help him understand. And there was no amount of coaching from me or sex that could heal his deepest needs. As his wife, I needed to adjust my tactics to what would best help my husband. Because what will work in one terrain may not be beneficial for the next. And you cannot fight spiritual battles with carnal equipment.

Instead of recognizing that my husband was in spiritual warfare, I internalized his distance as his lack of caring for me. After what seemed like constant rejection, I became vulnerable and susceptible to other men. It wasn't like I was actively seeking to have an affair. Instead, the advances I was oblivious to before became more noticeable to me. My guard was down. And I believe the men who sought me out could sense it.

For the weapons of our warfare are not carnal but mighty in God for pulling down strongholds...
~2 Corinthians 10:4

The door to my infidelity may have been opened by Leo, but that was a one-time rendezvous. Still, I was in a vulnerable state and it was another man whom I knew longer than Deion who took advantage of this.

In the thick of relationship troubles, you will feel a wide range of emotions and some of them can occur simultaneously. I loved Deion with all of me and I never thought I would be unfaithful to him. Though some of the roots of our relationship were underdeveloped or unnourished, I believe I was the best version of myself in that relationship as compared to who I was in any other relationship. Through all we had overcome together, we rode out waves of disappointments, personal failures, and triumphs. But it was not until the months leading up to our separation that I felt the loneliest. I loved Deion and was still in love with him, but I also felt empty. I felt he didn't want me. So I put on my combat boots by taking his rejection personally and going to battle to have my "needs" met.

But the situation did not require combat boots; it required the lighter treading of Chucks. Instead of internalizing his outward demonstrations as rejecting me, I now realize I should have paid more attention to his spirit. There may have been underlying issues affecting him but he felt uncomfortable sharing. Maybe he wanted to open up to me, but our relationship may have lacked the type of environment that would promote deep conversations. While I wanted to be his lover, Deion needed me as a friend. We had forgotten what it was like to be friends and this may have led to him closing his heart to me. I used to interrupt him during conversations to acknowledge what he was saying. I now see the value in active listening as a way to show someone you understand them. Without mumbling a word.

> *"I put on my combat boots by taking his rejection personally and going to battle to have my "needs" met."*

But when he passed out on the bedroom floor after the HandleBar, I had a lot to say. I sent a message to every single woman who had sent Deion a private message or text for his birthday. A night before, he had told me he no longer loved me and wanted a divorce. Tonight, we hung out with friends on the HandleBar to celebrate his birthday without as much as an affectionate touch from him to remain hopeful of our marriage. In a desperate move to reclaim the power I had lost in the relationship, I messaged those women to say that I was his wife and they now had permission to have him.

GOD, MY FATHER

Movie time with GPa 12.31.15

CHAPTER 17

A CLOSE FATHER

THE FIRST DAY OF MY reconciliation with God was the day after Deion's birthday. We woke up recuperating from the night before, he on the couch. Meanwhile, I awoke in our bed. Deion went to the store and retrieved some snacks for my hangover, but he was gone longer than usual. I began wondering if one of the women I texted the night before told him about my messages. If so, which one of them told him? I also wondered if his sobering up reminded him to follow through with his intentions from our argument a couple of nights ago. I may never know what happened during his trip to the store, but Deion returned home and freshened up.

WAR ROOM

While he was in the shower, I noticed several pairs of socks on our bed, which signaled he had no plans of returning any time soon. I immediately called the wife of the minister who married us. I desperately needed a word of hope and direction in saving my marriage. I needed someone to reassure me that this was a normal experience for couples. I needed help! The minister's wife listened as I told her about the argument where Deion said he wanted a divorce. The movie *War Room* had been in the movie theatre for several weeks and she strongly recommended we see it together. Deion and I went to the movies often and had read books on relationships in the past. So I figured he may have been open to this idea.

But I was wrong. After he got out of the shower, I asked Deion if he wanted to go to the movies and he said no and proceeded to get dressed for the day. His cold resolve was heartbreaking. He was usually open to seeing a movie for me. He had even been open to view similar movies like *Fireproof* and we'd discuss strategies to improve our relationship based off the lessons in these films. He didn't normally turn me down like this. I had only seen him behave that way toward others who had disappointed him, including his mother and some of his friends. Now, it was being directed toward me and I felt pushed away by his now hardened heart. It crushed me to know I used to have a place there but now I was being evicted for good. As he headed out the door, Deion said he was headed to his grandmother's. I don't know if I believed he was actually going there, but it didn't matter. I knew I NEEDED to see the film whether I saw it with him or without. I needed something to take my mind off the pain.

If you have ever seen *War Room*, you could imagine how much it resonated with me in my present state! The film portrays a marriage at a crossroads and how the power of prayer can transform us to affect a greater change in our relationships. As I sat alone in the dark movie theatre, I tried to avoid drawing unwanted attention. Silent tears fell from my face as I wept for the main character. Her story was my story. Her pain was my pain. Though the movie came to a hopeful resolution, my story had just begun. My truth was told in the first twenty minutes of the movie as my separation was initiated just moments before and I could not connect with the remainder of the story. By the end, however, I resolved to apply the principles the main character used to salvage her marriage. I didn't leave the theatre hoping for my husband to return or to even change his mind, but I knew the only thing I could transform about my situation was me.

From that moment, I was at war! Prayer was an intentional act each day as I committed to praying each morning. My prayers continued throughout the day as I needed strength just to complete the simplest tasks. I consumed scriptures like someone who had devoured food after years of famine. Uplifting scriptures were written on post-it notes throughout the apartment that was no longer occupied by my husband. One scripture I posted by the door leading out of the apartment reminding me to rely on God during this time was Philippians 4:19:

> *And my God shall supply all your need according to*
> *His riches in glory by Christ Jesus.*
> ~Philippians 4:19

I mean I really had no other choice. I used to rely on my own strength to get me through tough times. I'd push beyond exhaustion to work an extra hour or to follow through with a promise.

Now, I was in a state of powerlessness that was unfamiliar to me. I was totally dependent on God for ALL. There was nothing I could do. Nothing I could say to empower myself. I cried all the time. Imagine driving in constant rain for an hour and you turn on your windshield wipers, but you still cannot see. No matter how fast the wipers go, you're unable to see beyond the steering wheel from all the rain. That was my commute to and from work every day. For the two hours I spent on the road each day, my eyes poured like waterfalls and my eyelids could not clear the tears fast enough to enable me to see the road ahead. My emotions were all over the place at any given moment multiple times a day. This girl who was known for her smile and positive outlook on life had reached an all-time low that she could not easily bounce back from.

GOD, MY FATHER

Meanwhile, I found solace in the angels on earth that God surrounded me with including professional help. Prior to the separation, I contacted a therapist at the local seminary who was supposed to help Deion and me work through our issues. I immediately began going to counseling every week once Deion left. Like the *War Room*, I knew I needed to be there even if I went alone.

I was emotionally drained and didn't have the energy to give to anyone or to even reach out to others for help. During this time, I was focused on the restoration from within and trusted that God would be everything I needed. During some of my darkest days of the darkness, He told certain people to call or text me just to check in. These "angels" cared for, motivated, and inspired me with just enough strength to make it through the day or even the next moment.

Only a few of my "angels" knew what was going on because I was intentional about who I shared the news with. One person I felt comfortable being vulnerable with was my brother from another mother, Daniel. We had known each other since 1998 when my mother regained custody of my sister and me. We had not spoken since Deion and I got married, but I trusted his wisdom because he understood the foundation of my family in ways others would not. And he was a minister who could back up what he was saying with God's Word. It was like the best of both worlds because he both understood my motivations and could chastise me in Jesus's name all in the same breath. After several phone conversations during the separation, Daniel said "Sis, when you pray you can talk to God in a real way. You don't have to be perfect. He knows the real you and He loves you like a Father."

DATING DADDY

Like a Father?

What does that mean? What does that look like? As a fatherless daughter, I didn't have a clue how a father's love felt. I struggled with this and asked God for clarity.

The concept was above my head until one day I had an epiphany. I thought about my work with the extended school program in the affluent elementary school. I considered how much the parents of my students loved their children. They relentlessly advocated for and supported their children. I imagined these parents at a baseball game and the look of a proud father clapping for his kid every time he saw them on the field.

> "God is a proud father in the stands on high and I am His kid on the field of life."

It did not matter if the kid did well on the play or not; this father showed his support and amazement in the kid just because it was his kid.

Aha!!!

Is that how God is? He loves me that much? After thirty-one years without a consistent father figure, I was able to see God as a Father for the very first time! I used to think I was at a disadvantage because I grew up in a single parent home. I saw God as a distant provider who was only available in the time of trouble. I mistook church attendance and serving in ministry leadership as a sign of a closer relationship with the Creator. I believed in what I could see more than what I could not see and held a distrust in miracles in my own life. I had all these misconceptions of who God was and how He operated until I reached this dark season of my life.

God loves me THAT much?

Talk about an immediate shift in my perspective! I could now see GOD AS FATHER! God is a proud father in the stands on high and I am His kid on the field of life. Whether I make a good play or one that costs me the game, God STILL loves me. He is still proud of the girl He created and knew me from before I was formed in my mother's womb (Jeremiah 1:5). He not only loved me when I graduated from college or made choices as instructed by His Word, He also loves me in spite of the many mistakes I have made throughout my life and continue to make. My heavenly Father's love continues to surround me when I do not choose to follow His will or wait for his authority before making life-changing decisions. He loves me in spite of me!

BUDDING SPIRITUAL AUTHENTICITY

And now that Deion left, I could seek God without distraction. By November, I became a member of the church known for "leading people to a better life" and our church had a guest performer sing before Pastor preached. Though I was not familiar with his music, Travis Greene's song "Intentional" was popular to those who loved gospel music. "Intentional" didn't resonate with me as much as the other songs he sang during worship that Sunday. Following the service, I downloaded his album *The Hill* on my phone and played it every day. I listened to it as I prepared for work, during my commute, and once I returned home in the evening. I gravitated towards the song "Made a Way," which became a personal reminder that God can make a way out of anything. He has done so in the past and He most certainly will make a way during my separation from my husband.

The song that best describes my relationship with God during this time was his song "You Keep Me." The opening alone captured my own humble cry to my Father and my trust in His love to keep me. As I relied on God to sustain me, I moved through the blaming stage of my marital separation to considering my role in the relationship. In those first days and weeks I had cried, "He left!" like a song that skips repeatedly and is unattended to. But now my cries were no longer, "HE LEFT!" I realized there were harsh words that were better left unsaid and situations that I took the lead on for selfish reasons. The guilt of all I had done or didn't realize was harmful to my marriage weighed heavily upon me.

> "Once I became more authentic in my prayer life, I experienced His peace like never before."

Seeking God was the only option to healing my broken heart. The pain and emptiness I felt from the separation was like someone had violently pulled my heart from my chest. It was as raw as raw could get. Nothing else could heal me the way I needed to be healed. It couldn't be drinking. It couldn't be shopping or promiscuity. Nothing could fill the void I knew only God could fill.

My prayer life was transformed during the separation. My brother Daniel shared with me that I can pray to my Heavenly Father about how I truly feel. He said to pray to God about my shortcomings even if it meant praying, "God, I know Your word says to do this, but I'm not there yet." My prayers went from sounding like the Lord's Prayer to "God, this is what is going on…please help me…I trust Your Will…help me love this man more like You even if our relationship doesn't change." Once I became more authentic in my prayer life, I experienced His peace like never before. Yes, I was an emotional wreck like anyone else who has experienced a separation or divorce, but His peace reassured me everything would get better. I couldn't see it for myself, but God surrounded me with His love through my "angels." I wanted to fall apart. I wanted to not continue living through the pain, but He kept me.

JUSTICE OF THE PEACE

God kept me even when I discovered Deion had done the unthinkable. We had been separated for over a month and a half when I received a postcard in the mail from the post office that I missed a certified letter. I didn't think much of it because I had not ordered anything that would require my signature. The next day, I came home to a piece of mail from "Somebody and Somebody Else," which set off an alarm because I knew it was a law firm. When I opened the mail, the first lines read something like, "Even if you chose to dissolve your marriage or it was decided for you…choose us." I froze! Had Deion filed for divorce? This law firm had to know something I didn't know. Why else would they send a letter like that to me? They could have only known if Deion filed and they obtained my information, I thought.

I took a couple of deep breaths and called Deion. I calmly asked him if he had filed for divorce. He explained that he had and we talked for the next hour or two. I don't remember what was said, maybe because I was in a daze of disbelief. This was like the final act of severing the tie between us. When we got off the phone, I immediately called my therapist and left her an inaudible voicemail chopped up in tears from the recent news. After I hung up, my friend Lily randomly texted to see how I was doing. She had known about the separation and regularly recommended I focus on self-care. When I responded that Deion filed for divorce, she called immediately. She was so loving and reassuring as I told her what had just happened. She helped calm my tears of hysteria. It was as if God took care of me before I laid my head down because as soon as Lily hung up, my therapist called and helped me process what I could to help me sleep that evening.

DATING DADDY

Still, I did not want the divorce. Deion and I had not lived together for almost two months and I found it too hard to talk to him, but something within me wanted to stay in the marriage. Despite our situation, I believed God could restore us and that our marriage could become a ministry. If we were able to ride out this storm, we could conquer anything. We could encourage other couples that they too can survive anything together. But I could not ignore what I believe God told me before I learned Deion filed for divorce. In a voice so clear, I could hear God tell me, "Let go." I wasn't sure I heard him clearly and began asking God what He wanted me to let go of. Unforgiveness? Hurt? I was not quite sure what God wanted me to release. About a week later, I received that advertisement from the divorce lawyers.

With what strength I had, I returned to my CrossFit box, which was now renamed a fit club with many fitness options for all interests. In the past, I had been in and out of the box due to our fluctuating finances, but now I had no other choice. I borrowed money to get back in the gym. It would prove to be an investment worthy of the sacrifice and my workouts had a new meaning for me. I could channel my frustrations. Every workout allowed me to release whatever intense emotion I was experiencing in that moment as I focused on each kettlebell swing, run, lift, and jump as prescribed by Coach Red. On days I didn't think I needed to workout, my spirit was so low. My friend Chrisette noticed this and encouraged me to keep going if for no other reason but to have a relatively good day.

Deion's absence was bittersweet. On one hand, it was so unbearable I felt like I would break down at any given moment. I took days off of work when the pain was too intolerable. When I did work, I avoided as much unnecessary conversation as I could with students and colleagues throughout the day. On the other hand, I was now free to seek the relationship with God I had long suppressed because of Deion's and my different beliefs. I no longer had to entertain some of the people he associated with. I was free to be Shavonne for the first time since the discovery of Deion's affair. It was a devastating freedom, to say the least.

CHAPTER 18

A FATHER'S JOY: DAUGHTER'S RESTORATION

IN 2007, MY FRIEND CHRISTYN'S father referred to me as the "prodigal daughter" after I returned home following several nights away. Without much knowledge of the biblical reference, I was simply content he accepted me as one of his children. I appreciated my surrogate parents' generosity for allowing me to stay in their vastly beautiful, multi-generational home after I graduated from undergrad, the size of which was larger than anything I could ever imagine. Like the little orphan Annie, it was a humbling experience. Most nights were spent at Leo's house because I wanted to avoid being a burden. As the years passed, however, my curiosity about the story of the prodigal son grew. It was not until this season of life, nearly eight years later, that it all made sense. It made perfect sense.

THE PROMISE

In Luke 15, Jesus shares the well-known parable of the prodigal son. This story demonstrates the unending love a father has for his children regardless of their choices in life. In the parable, there were two brothers who were guaranteed an inheritance from their father. The eldest son was responsible and loyal to the father. If the eldest brother lived in today's times, he would have been the straight A student who never got into any sort of trouble. The younger brother was quite the opposite. He was a bit more of a risk taker and had a bold sense of entitlement. Jesus said the younger son asked for the inheritance from his father in advance. The father granted the younger son his wish.

Similarly, I feel that I knew what was promised to me from God. I believe my Heavenly Father revealed to me years ago that I would receive the blessing of marriage. In the years between the revelation and my marriage to Deion, God had been preparing me. At one point, I studied Proverbs 31 in depth and God revealed several things to me about being the ideal wife. He also taught me patience through the story of Sarah and Abraham. I learned the importance of seeking God for fulfillment through my study of the Samaritan woman at the well. These are just a few of the ways God was preparing my heart and mind for marriage.

God had even given living examples of His promise to me. When Deion and I met, I was twenty-six years old. I was seeing waves of friends, sorority sisters, and associates who were getting married. I had attended numerous showers and gatherings that led up to these ceremonies and depleted the little income I had for gifts from their registries. This wave of weddings was followed by yet another wave of couples who were now expanding their families, which meant there were now baby showers to attend. I prided myself in being one of the few women who did not mind going to a wedding without a date, but the thought of being in a committed relationship did cross my mind—it just did not consume me. I was genuinely happy for the couples who were expanding their families. I didn't feel threatened or insecure about this as I patiently awaited His promise to manifest itself in my life. He not only revealed my promise but God showed me a glimpse of what the future held for me through the life changes of the people in my circle.

In my spiritual walk, I behaved much like the older son in Luke 15. As long as I was single, God was my first priority and the center of my life. I went to church regularly, served in ministry and in the community, and grew in my knowledge of the Bible. I made "responsible" Christian decisions, which I now realize was my way of trying to earn good points with God.

Once I met Deion, my behavior became more like the younger son. I thought this was the relationship that would manifest God's promise to me. Marriage was the inheritance I was to receive from my Heavenly Father and I asked for it to be with Deion. I approached God in a way that one of my former co-workers would say, "Ask for forgiveness, not for permission." I did not seek God's approval of Deion in advance. I didn't even ask if God thought I was ready. Instead, I asked God to show me if this was the man I was supposed to be with—only after he proposed.

Be careful what you ask for because you just might get it. When I sought God's clarity after we were engaged, I did not expect what came next. Soon after, dreams and revelations came to me that may have been warnings or God's way of showing me my answer. But I didn't trust them. I wanted His original promise for me and believed Deion was who I was supposed to spend my life with because he proposed with a ring. Had there been more obvious signs before the proposal that things would not work out, I may have left the relationship long before it reached that point. But because these signs came during the months leading to the altar, I saw them as tests of my commitment more than a way of escape.

PLAYING IN THE PIGPEN

But fathers have the difficult task of choosing when to protect their children from hurting themselves or allowing them to learn lessons the hard way. Sometimes, a father will prevent you from making mistakes that will damage you. Other times, they will allow you to go through your experience with a watchful eye, anxiously awaiting your return to your good senses. Like a good father, God will allow us to continue our own way to learn important lessons for ourselves. God revealed to me long ago that I would be married and have a family of my own. I don't think He told me not to marry Deion, but I believe He did allow me to marry him for the lessons I'm sharing with you through my story.

After the prodigal son squandered his inheritance and the severe famine engulfed the country, he took a job tending to pigs. No longer was he living like the son of a father who had more than enough, but he had been reduced to work and low living that was beneath even the servants at his father's home. Abundance had always been his at his father's house, as well as the servants' too, with plenty of fine food and leftovers for everyone—but now the son understood what lack felt like. He had reached such a low point in his life that he even yearned after what the pigs ate. Imagine going from opulent feasts to now happily downing some pig food. We may be quick to say this is something we could never do, but you never know what you would do to stay afloat in "survival mode."

In my marriage, when I had nothing left to give and the joy dried up, I sought things outside of it to fill the emptiness. I may not have tended to pigs or saw their feed as desirable, but I did behave in ways that were not a part of my character or who I saw myself as. I've laid many of my shortcomings out in this book, but I believe I'm not the only one who has done things I'm not proud of. I dare you to reflect on how you may have fallen short after experiencing a drought in your relationship or following repeated hardships in your own life. Once you are removed from the situation, it becomes clear that who you were in "survival mode" is not the same person as who you are when times are good. Acknowledging this can fill you with grace and relief from trying to be perfect.

Striving for perfection can lead to self-loathing when you fall short. I wanted to be the trophy wife who could take care of home, support my husband, and looked amazing at all times. When nothing I did kept my husband happy, I felt like a failure. I wondered why I wasn't enough. Even after he left, I found myself repeating in tears, "Why didn't he fight for me?" Why didn't he fight his feelings that were telling him to leave our marriage or fight for what our marriage represented? My biggest act of forgiveness was to forgive myself. I had to forgive myself for not telling the truth about how I felt with Deion and for walking on eggshells to "protect" him. I had to forgive myself for being unfaithful in my marriage. Most of all, I had to forgive myself for thinking I was on this journey all by myself.

Whew! When I let go of all the real and perceived expectations I could not live up to, God was able to heal me. When I was still holding on to the belief that I was perfect, God could not do anything for me. But when I was broken, I was able to yield to Him like never before. Sometimes we say we trust God, only to get in the way by trying to "help Him" answer our prayers a little quicker and in our favor. But it is when you're at the end of yourself that God can make the most unimaginable things happen for you. It takes complete surrender. We must surrender the idea that we know what is best for us. We need to be patient with the process as only His timing will perfect our character. Unfortunately, it took a total beat-down by life for me to surrender completely. And like the son in the parable, this prodigal daughter returned home.

A PENITENT HOMECOMING

I have never been as defeated in my entire life as I was after my husband left. I would not have known what to do on my own, but I believe God used the movie *The War Room* to prepare me for this season. It helped me focus my energies on seeking a closer relationship with Him. From September through December 2015, it was just God and me as I spent the last few months alone in the apartment that was once occupied by my husband and me for the duration of our marriage.

In the fog of the separation, I could not see anything except that my husband left our marriage. To make matters worse, he looked disgusted at the sight of me the one or two times we met up during the separation. Cold words were said. Still I believed our marriage could recover. I was not ready to let go of the union that brought out some of my best qualities and gave me much growth. It was during the relationship that I fell in love with CrossFit, was supported through the battles that only Deion knew about, and graduated with an advanced degree in education. The memories of the good times overshadowed the severe insecurity I developed from feeling inadequate. Like my relationship with my biological father, I had accomplished so much despite the pain that was going on at home in my relationship with Deion. Yet, his absence was a clear indication of my powerlessness to change things.

At the same time, I was becoming aware of how I had fallen short in my relationship with God. I reached an all-time low and, like the prodigal son, humbly returned to my Father. I know this could be controversial for some. Why would a "gracious Heavenly Father" allow us to experience heartbreak, disillusionment, or any other uncomfortable feeling if He loves us so much? I don't know. What I do know is that without it, I would not have been as receptive to Him. I would not have been open to receiving the everyday miracles and revelations He showed me throughout my healing process. Most important, I would not be here sharing my story because I lost the will to live a long time ago.

> *"This was the worst thing that could have happened to me but it was also the best thing that could have happened because of the woman I became in the process."*

Furthermore, my brokenness allowed me to experience God as my father after many years without my own. I truly grasped what it meant to have a father during my final months in that apartment. As He did with the father of the prodigal son, God had allowed me to make my own choices and that included my choice in marrying Deion. When I prayed to God during our engagement, He did not approve or disapprove of the marriage. Instead, I discovered Deion's unfaithfulness but moved forward anyway. Later, God surprised me when I said the prayer of desperation, "Our marriage cannot continue like this."

Well, I didn't think God would take it literally!

But when I returned to Him, I could feel God's pleasure and presence like never before. All my masks no longer fit, my heart was open, and I could not "perform" to save my life. Like the prodigal son, I humbly returned home to a Father who was just happy to have me back! Our wavering journey began years ago, but I had reached the point of true reliance on God. Riley, Chrisette, and Kori witnessed the constant tears, insecurities, and pain during my transformation. They each said that this was the worst thing that could have happened to me but it was also the best thing that could have happened because of the woman I became in the process.

A GRANDFATHER'S JOY

Though Uncle Phil Collins was the first family member to know of my separation, it was my GPa's sense of humor and consistency that helped me maintain and regain a sense of normalcy. Most weekends, we would meet up for a movie date, which dated back to my return home following my undergraduate commencement in December 2006.

GPa has always been around, but it wasn't until high school that we turned over a new leaf in our relationship. Before, he enabled my mom's addiction, but when his life turned around he became a great father figure to me. He attended every performance in high school and celebrated all my accomplishments. He believed in my dreams probably more than I did. It was never a question of who would walk me down the aisle because my grandfather had become my dad to me by stepping in to help my sister and me when my mom could not.

When considering family members who fill in the gap, we often think of the women who step up rather than the men. Author Aaron Smith thought otherwise and gave voice to African American grandfathers who, with their wives, served as primary caregivers to their grand- and great-grandchildren. Smith noted, "These grandfathers do not fit the societal perception of black men who abandon and neglect their families with seemingly little regard for their young children." He also states that grandparents often provide this type of "parental" care when a relative is incarcerated, suffers from a drug or alcohol addiction, or is otherwise unable to raise his own children.

Same was true with my experience. GPa often filled in the gap when Mom could not. What makes our situation differ from the research was that he married a woman other than my maternal grandmother. Imagine the adjustments, the accommodations, the sacrifices GPa's wife made for us while he ensured we were doing well. To this day, she supports him and our weekly dates at the movies.

It was during the movie dates following the separation that GPa became aware of my marital troubles. I wanted to open up to my mother, but as you may remember, she had just checked into the hospital and it became too difficult to not tell GPa. Every Saturday, he'd give me a big hug and ask how his favorite granddaughter was doing, followed by an inquiry about Deion. I don't remember which weekend I told him the truth, but I guess the heartbreak was written all over my face. I didn't realize my sadness impacted him so deeply. He, like most people who knew me, always saw me smile, but for the first time in my life I did not pretend to be okay. My life as I knew it was falling apart and all I wanted was to regain a sense of normalcy.

During the months of my separation, going to the movies with GPa provided just that. Normalcy. But it was also a time when I bonded with his wife. She spoke into my spirit and gave me instructions for self-care without being intrusive. (You would never imagine the insensitive things people say to you when you are already feeling low.) Where GPa made efforts to cheer me up through his humor, Grandma was supportive of me in a way that only a woman would know how.

By the time Deion and I went to court for our mediation in December 2015, I had a peace within that reassured me everything would be all right. Initially, I wanted to delay the process in the hope that my marriage would be restored. When I saw Deion that day, we had not seen each other for over two months and the look on his face showed that he was hurting as bad as I was. After we appeared before the judge, I asked him if he really wanted to move forward with the divorce, to which he replied yes. I struggled with his response and within an hour or so we divided what little assets we had to move the process along.

Later that month, my happiest moment was not when I started to smile again. It was when my GPa SAW me smile again. Until this point, he did all he could to cheer me up and encourage me, but I was stuck in a place it seemed I would never break free from. That particular movie date, I will never forget the smile on his face as we bought popcorn and he said, "It's good to see my granddaughter happy again!" I won't say I was smiling from ear to ear, but I was no longer in denial. My marriage was ending. As I was coming to terms with that, I began to experience God's peace and it was as if GPa's contentment represented God's approval for my return to Him.

Though my circumstances were not perfect, this transformative journey has connected me to you. I may never know where you are on your journey, but know that God loves you unconditionally. Our Heavenly Father will not force himself on you. Though He accepts you with open arms, His love will transform you from what you were before. The prodigal son left the lavish life and all that he indulged in to return home. Likewise, a closer relationship with our Father will require a separation from those addictions, unhealthy habits, toxic relationships, and anything else that caused a chasm between you and Him in the first place. But don't worry, you have a loving father who is awaiting your return.

CHAPTER 19

SHADOW OF DEATH

AT THE TOP OF THE 2016, I found peace through God knowing that everything would be okay. Things could only go uphill from here and the worst part of the experience had come to pass. Or so I thought. As I shook off the dust of 2015 and working through my heartache, I thought I'd learned all the lessons God had for me through this experience. Normalcy resumed with my return to CrossFit, going to church, therapy, and the Saturday matinees with GPa. Oddly, there was one particular movie I saw with him that would resonate with me the most.

THE REVENANT

On Saturday, January 9, 2016, GPa and I met up to catch the movie *The Revenant,* a brutal story of grief, vengeance and survival starring Leonardo DiCaprio as Hugh Glass, a frontiersman exploring the uncharted wilderness in 1823. As I watched the film, I wondered how DiCaprio's character survived all that he faced and lived longer than his character in *The Titanic*. After a while, I was curious about the meaning behind the title name and broke the movie cardinal rule. With my phone held against my chest, I secretly turned it on to look up the definition of the movie title midway through the film.

> rev·e·nant – noun 1. a person who has returned, especially supposedly from the dead.

Having witnessed all that Hugh Glass faced by the middle of the movie, I doubted he would be able to recover. For those of you who have seen the movie, you know what I am talking about. For those of you who have not, I do not spoil movies so you'll have to see it for yourself. Let's just say that Leo's character suffered life threatening injuries, severe attacks, and heart wrenching loss on his journey. Nonetheless, the definition of revenant reassured me he would be victorious in the end. Still, I wondered,

How could ANYONE come back from ALL of that??

I spoke too soon. The movie was not only based off a true story that seemed to be exaggerated for the big screen, but it appeared in its seemingly exaggerated glory to portend my own revenant experience.

The next day, January 10, it snowed more than it had all winter and I awoke to a call from my mother. She informed me that her brother Mike had passed earlier that morning after his bout with throat cancer. Our family expected his death to occur at any moment because he had been on home hospice after his prognosis. Still, it's not easy to deal with the passing of a loved one so I prepared myself to pick up my mother. Several of her other siblings were headed to Uncle Mike's house and his body was picked up before I arrived to pick up mom and Aunt Pat, my sister's aunt. When I arrived, she said she wanted to check on GMa. I obliged.

We sat at GMa's house for an hour or two before I drove Mom and Aunt Pat home. On our way, Mom asked if we could stop by her Uncle Moses' house, my GMa's only brother. Luckily, I knew how to get to Uncle Moses' home because my mom was too grief stricken to give directions. I had taken her to visit him several times before in the last few weeks.

As I turned onto the street, I saw a police car parked in front of the house where Moses lived and asked mom if she saw it too. She immediately started crying, "Oh, he's dead too!!" I tried to reassure Mom not to assume something so grim. As I continued down the narrow street, we saw a lady on the porch and my mother jumped out of the moving car toward her. I stopped the car in the street and rolled down the window to hear what the woman had to say.

She asked, "Are you here for Moses?"

My mother had gotten closer to the porch by now when the lady said the unthinkable.

"He's dead."

Right there in the front yard, my mom flipped out! Two family deaths in one day! My mother had lost one of her eldest brothers and only maternal uncle on the same day. I lost my Uncle Mike and Uncle Moses, who especially meant a lot to me because he my birthday twin. If we did not talk any other day of the year, we at least spoke on our birthdays. His celebrity lookalike was basketball playing, vampire slaying Wesley Snipes. Though he was the life the party at our family functions, Uncle Moses could minister to you about God during a card game in a room full of cigarette smoke.

Aunt Pat asked me to open the back door of my car where she sat bound by the childproof locks. As I got out of the car to free Aunt Pat, I was overtaken by grief and fell out in the middle of the street in tears. I cried and wanted to scream so loud. I probably did but I cannot remember. It was like life had stripped me to the bare bones.

How much more could I lose?

How could God allow me to be picked apart when I had nothing left to give up?

Finally, I was able to walk around the car to free Aunt Pat. We learned we had just arrived before the coroner. I frantically called my cousin because I knew she'd be the next of kin who was not at our Uncle Mike's house from that morning. Then, I called Deion and the phone rang until it finally went to voicemail.

I finally went into the house, but could not stop crying. His body was two rooms away and I could not contain myself. Aunt Pat, my cousin, and one of Uncle Moses's toothless roommates tried to console me, but the dams of their hugs and embrace could not slow down the floodgates of my tears or my growing grief migraine. The most vivid image from Uncle Moses's house on that day was the moment I stood in view of the coroner as my uncle's body was lifted and placed on the stretcher in the black bag. When I saw this, my sorrow intensified yet again, striking me down on the floor.

Once his body was taken away, we all went our separate ways. Somehow I made it to my friend Riley's apartment by early evening. My head throbbed from all the tears and tension. For the rest of the evening Riley and Chrisette allowed me to pour out my heart under their loving care.

BEYOND BROKEN

The next morning, Monday, January 11, I returned home drained from the day before and from lack of sleep. Throughout the morning, Chrisette and Riley checked in on me through a series of group texts amongst the three of us. Less than twenty-four hours ago, I lost two uncles in the midst of an unwanted separation from my husband.

And of all days, one of our mutual friends asked for the name of a divorce lawyer through an early morning text??? I was livid!

I told Chrisette and Riley about this and they were in disbelief as well, but this grand offense was nothing compared to what happened next. Less than two hours later I received the call that pushed me over the edge. It was a representative from the court who said, "There is one final paper to sign to end it all."

Really???

The clerk barely greeted me over the phone before she gave instructions for finalizing my divorce! Words cannot describe the moments of insanity that followed.

I broke...

Immediately, my inner dialogue sounded like a crowded room during a dinner party.

"I'm going to show you!"

"...don't do anything out of anger..."

"I can't control anything else! Why not?"

Until finally, all the voices stopped and all I could hear was, *"I'm done."*

With that, grief took over. Shavonne had left the room. Grief took my car keys and drove immediately to the courthouse. Grief got on the elevator and picked up the document indicating I was never served the original summons. Grief walked to the nearest bank a couple of blocks away and obtained a notary for the document. Grief roamed back to the courthouse and submitted the document to the court clerk. And grief sped to the emergency therapy appointment that I originally scheduled after leaving Uncle Moses' yesterday but was now late for due to my life-changing detour.

After my intensely emotional session, I took a two or three hour nap before my friend Naomi came by with my favorite ice cream. She was unaware of how close my divorce was to being finalized.

Kori, who I was staying with, was only aware of the deaths in my family. She returned home after work on a mission to cheer me up. Kori went straight to the kitchen to work her magic and offered me a glass of wine while Naomi and I talked in the living room. At first, I refused because I knew I should avoid drinking under my extremely emotional state. Don't get me wrong—I was far from a teetotaler and I had an occasional drink every now and then. But when I checked the status of our divorce online, I found that my marriage was officially dissolved and I swallowed the wine like water.

Throughout the separation and pending divorce, I refused to post anything on social media about the issues in my relationship. But that evening, I wrote a status on Facebook

"Rest in peace Uncle Mike.

Rest in peace Uncle Moses.

Rest in peace my marriage."

Almost immediately, my inbox and status received a lot of attention. Within twenty-four minutes, at least twenty people reached out to me directly on social media and by phone to encourage me. Bothered by the attention it drew, I took the post down and returned to the company of my friends who were still oblivious to what I saw on the court's website.

All I knew was that I wanted to drink myself into extinction. I wanted to get to the point where I was in a constant state of unconsciousness. I didn't want to feel anything. And once I got there, I wanted yet another drink. In this very moment, I felt like life was punching me in the chest, tamping down on my heart while it was already in the intensive care unit.

I had two glasses of wine that felt like I had a bottle or two when I noticed some missed calls. It was my brother from another mother, Daniel. He called several times but I didn't pick up. I didn't want to be inconsiderate of Kori and Naomi's company as they were there to support me. Yet, he was the only person I felt comfortable talking to that evening because I knew whatever he had to say was out of love.

Once Kori went to bed and Naomi left to go home, I returned his call.

Drunk.

I told him what had gone on and he listened attentively. Usually, we would be on the phone for hours and it would mostly be him talking. Tonight, however, he listened as his Sis poured out her heart. I told him about my uncles' deaths and about the details of being in the house as Uncle Moses's body was taken out. I told him about how I didn't want the divorce and now it is final. Other than that, I don't remember what else I shared with Daniel, but he listened attentively and strategically interjected to pray over me.

Why did he have to pray while I was drunk? Talk about a guilt trip!

Immediately, I tried to get on my knees in reverence but I was too drunk to hold that position. With my eyes closed, the room was spinning uncontrollably! So I stood up and walked around the condo as he prayed. Once he was done, he spoke words of encouragement to me and said that he loved me before we got off the phone and I crashed on the couch for the night.

NUMB

The next two weeks that followed were dizzying. My family was in the process of planning two funerals and my mother was identified as the next of kin for Uncle Moses's arrangements. In his final days, Mom visited him regularly and had an idea of how he wanted to be buried and whom to contact to participate in the ceremony. I did my best to assist her, but Mom coordinated a beautiful going-home service for Uncle Moses even while she grieved the loss of her brother Mike.

My now ex-husband served in the Honor Guard, which performs flag ceremonies for the funerals of military personnel. When he first joined, I spent countless hours with him as he practiced folding the American flag. My biggest fear was that he would be at one of the funerals. Both of my uncles served in the military but it was Uncle Mike who served in the same branch as Deion. Fortunately, he was not there on this day but one of the honor guards was someone who frequently worked with Deion during some of the funeral services I had attended.

On the Wednesday following Uncle Mike's funeral, Mom'ela had a doctor's appointment for something that was unclear to me. For most of my life, I have known Mom to be a hypochondriac and I thought she was being overdramatic about her health condition. This time though, something within me pushed me to go to the hospital after work. When I arrived, I saw Mom in bed in the weakest condition I have ever seen her. Unsure of why she was in the hospital in the first place, I asked the medical professionals for clarity. They said the surgeon had removed a mass from her chest through her ribcage! I went immediately into caretaker mode. Seeing my mother like this, I could not leave her alone. I called a friend, Shawnee, who lived near the hospital and asked for a pair of sweatpants to sleep in for the night. To help Mom relax, I combed her hair and braided it as best as I could. (My sister is the cosmetologist, not me.) But there was no other place I was going to be.

Over the days that followed, her condition did not seem to improve and I checked on her each day she was in the hospital. She was released on Saturday but contracted pneumonia and was readmitted by Sunday. Thankfully, her brother, the one who reminds me of El DeBarge, and his wife visited her when I was unable to be by her bedside. Once I arrived to the hospital, it wasn't long before I witnessed a painful episode when she could not breathe. Even the nurse could not provide relief to ease my mother's excruciating pain. I felt my anxiety escalate and I slowly made my way to the bathroom in the suite to avoid Mom seeing my tears.

DATING DADDY

I could not lose my mother, too!

I'd already lost my marriage, Uncle Mike, and Uncle Moses a couple of weeks ago. I did not have it in me to cope with another loss. Again, how much could a person take? I felt myself sinking into a state of numbness.

It took some time, but the pain medications finally provided some relief for my mom. Once Mom's condition stabilized, my aunt and uncle left the hospital to return home. Mom had not eaten much that day and I knew there was one thing that could help change her mood: music.

I played the Michael Cooper station on Pandora and Mom cheered up almost instantly. She used to play him on repeat at home when I was growing up and I could see her dancing throughout our apartment. In this moment, I hoped for even a semblance of that happiness in her hospital room. With each song, she became more cheerful. When her dinner arrived, she ate over half of it, which was more than she had eaten all day. For the past week, I was beyond exhausted from the funerals to Mom's condition and hadn't really slept a full night so I knew I would be returning home that evening. I waited until she appeared to be drifting off to sleep before I left the hospital.

Mom's final nights in the hospital were eventful. First, we learned her eldest brother was admitted to the same hospital on the same day and was in a room a few floors up. That same evening, Mom had a manic episode after receiving too much medicine. She called my sister and me at three or four in the morning frantic because she didn't know where she was and assumed the nurse she saw in her room cut open her chest. She had completely forgotten about her surgery less than a week ago and it took over an hour to calm her down. Restless, I got a few moments of sleep before getting up and preparing for my daily commute to work, which was an hour away.

BACK TO THE BASICS

And let us not grow weary while doing good, for in due season we shall reap if we do not lose heart
~Galatians 6:9

Broken.
Beyond broken.
Now numb.

Around the time Mom'ela was released from the hospital, she received news from the doctors regarding the mass they removed from her ribcage. She was diagnosed with Hodgkin's Lymphoma, which is a form of cancer that attacks the immune system and makes it difficult for the body to fight infections. Realizing life is short, I assumed responsibility for taking care of Mom and ensuring her needs were met. Still traumatized from my own life events, I vowed to visit her Sundays after church. Even with this commitment, I often lacked the energy to stay for more than a few hours before having an anxiety attack from thinking of the umpteen traumas I experienced in the last few months.

How could I move forward? How could any good come from this? I did not see how I could be of any good to anyone else, especially because I could not take care of myself. How could I even try to see outside of my own needs to care for another? I was less concerned with reaping material goods than I was about the restoration of my spirit, of the joy I once had.

During the therapy session the following week, I expressed how exhausted I was from all that was going on and my eagerness for brighter days. As I spoke, my therapist listened attentively and validated my feelings. She said that I've dealt with a lot of loss in such a short time span. There was a moment of silence as she took a breath and asked some questions that led to my life changing epiphany. She knew I did CrossFit and asked me what my coaches would say to me during difficult workouts. As if in a daze, I slowly answered that they would push me to keep going, that there's more within me, and to remember the basics while lifting heavier weights.

Remember the basics….

They instruct us to lift the lighter weight as if it were heavier weights, stressing the point that the same techniques we use to lift the lighter weights will help us when the bar is loaded with more plates.

> **"I had to treat it like a squat. When you're down with the loaded bar on your shoulders, there is no other direction to go but upwards."**

In that moment, I had the "aha moment" of all aha moments! I thought about the new practices I had established during my separation such as daily prayer, reading the Bible and following devotional plans. When times grew tough, I learned to stop and become present in the moment. When I felt myself becoming anxious or overwhelmed, I took deep breaths or short walks to clear my mind. All these "little" techniques I used to cope over the past five months became the basics I could implement to help me now.

My own revenant experience was at its turning point. I no longer expected life to get easier, but I did expect to be stronger because of it. I realized God had already equipped me with all I needed for the journey ahead. Each trial and test may have felt like the weight of the world was on my shoulders, but I had to treat it like a squat. When you're down with the loaded bar on your shoulders, there is no other direction to go but upwards. I had to brace myself with prayer, surround myself by positive people, and repeat words of affirmation to overcome the darkest season of my adulthood.

With that, I focused my energies into training to compete as an Olympic weightlifter. I registered with the USA Weightlifting organization and arranged my work schedule as much as I could around the class times. As a novice to the sport, there was so much I needed to learn, but the journey would prove so many things about my internal strength—more than I could ever imagine.

History could have repeated itself. I realized there was a connection between the events of January 1996 and January 2016. In 1996, my mother lost her two brothers within twenty-four hours and she turned to drugs to cope. She felt isolated by the experience and found it hard to take care of us while processing her grief. Twenty years later, in January 2016, I completely understood the depth of her grief through the losses of my marriage, Uncle Mike and Uncle Moses within twenty-four hours. I was headed down my own path of destruction.

> *"History could have repeated itself."*

Much like David, I felt like I was walking "through the valley of the shadow of death..." (Psalm 23:4). Death and the possibility of death surrounded me. In my valley, I walked a thin line between indulging in destructive behaviors and seeking God's guidance through it all. Thank God I was surrounded by friends and did not live alone during this season. I could only imagine how far my vulnerability would have driven me if I hadn't been surrounded by their love. I was constantly reminded that God had something major on the other side of this. He just had to—but first I had to learn how to let go.

CHAPTER 20

LEARNING TO LET GO

HOW DO YOU GET CLOSURE when you experience abrupt abandonment? It would be easier if you could just see the person face to face and talk out your issues. If you could just sit down one more time, you could at least try to correct your mistakes and rectify the wrong in your failed relationship. But sometimes that's not an option. Whether the connection ceased due to physical death, abandonment, or another reason, the lingering pain and confusion of unanswered questions are left hanging in the balance of your mind. I cannot speak for everyone, but I began finding closure in the following ways.

ACCEPTING MANNA: TAKE ONE DAY AT A TIME

Before addressing how to let go, however, I'd like to talk about the stage between having the thing you once had and the land of your new normal. I'd like to call this the "manna" season after the Old Testament story of the children of Israel's journey from their enslavement in Egypt to the abundance of the Promised Land. They spent forty years in the wilderness between Egypt and the Promised Land and God made daily provisions for the Israelites, including manna to eat. Every day, the Israelites had to learn to trust God as they were given only what they needed for sustenance each day. During my wilderness experience, God delivered manna through the outpouring of offers for free food and encouraging words from friends and family even while they were unaware of what had transpired.

But my "manna season" represented more than my daily need for food. It included the daily word that would get me through my moments of hopelessness. It was in the moments I could not see my way through the fog of life that I received direction to see my circumstance more clearly. On November 1, 2015, the pastor of the church where "Jesus is exalted and the word is explained" preached a sermon titled, "Before You Say I Quit," as a part of a six-week series on relationships. I had not attended this church in years, but it was fate that I found this sermon when I did. In it, the pastor explained God's original purposes for marriage and how He permitted divorce due to the hardheartedness of men. The pastor shared with the congregation the concessions the Apostle Paul made for divorce, including abandonment by a spouse.

When I heard the sermon, I still believed my marriage could be restored but was surprised when I was made aware Deion had filed for divorce just a few days later. By this point, I felt I really didn't know who he was. How could this man whom I once shared so many good times with become so cold and want to abandon all we had? An internal battle ensued between my desire to be patient and ride this wave out, and choosing to let him go. Paul says that if an unbeliever of Christ leaves the marriage to let them go because God desires for His children to have peace. Not only that, but how can I be sure if I could do anything to change him (1 Corinthians 7:15-16)? I read and reread that scripture over and over until I accepted I may not have been able to change Deion's heart at all.

But didn't I say this was a manna season? God knew what I needed to hear to keep me going during this tumultuous time. The following Sunday, I decided to attend the church in person and the pastor preached a sermon titled, "Since You Said I Quit." *Did he know I was just made aware of my pending divorce?*

It would be impossible for him to know the details of my life!

In this fifth part of the series, pastor's message focused on seeking God's restoration following the end of a marriage. "Since You Said I Quit" focused on the story of Ruth (Ruth 1:3-5) when she became single again following the death of her husband. But Ruth was not the only one who was dealing with being single again. This plight was shared with both her sister-in-law Orpah and their mother-in-law Naomi. In the story, Ruth's mother-in-law Naomi lost her husband and her two sons and made the decision to return to her hometown. Orpah stayed in Moab to increase her chances of finding a new husband; meanwhile, Ruth decided to follow Naomi to develop herself in faith. Likewise, we must be intentional with our next moves at the end of relationships. You do not have to figure it all out today; just take one day at a time.

SEEK WISE COUNSEL: THERAPY

One of the most significant ways I began learning how to let go of my marriage was through seeking professional help. Therapy allowed me to process everything in a way that my family, friends and loved ones could not help me to do. It aided in my healing significantly and helped me to open up in a way I never had before. Prior to the separation, I would realize things that bothered me, but I would continue through life as if I was unaffected. As a result, I gave off the image that I was always well and that my life was "perfect." To others, everything seemed ideal with my life. In less than a four-month time period, I obtained everything that many women wanted: I married the man of my dreams and graduated with an advanced degree before my thirtieth birthday. Even *I* believed I was fortunate to experience so much good in my life, but when Deion left, I was forced to deal with the dissolving of my marriage as well as all the issues

I thought I'd dealt with in the past, but never truly resolved. It was as if his departure was a catalyst bringing all the hurt I from childhood experiences to the surface. It became critical to seek out help in dealing with this heavy load.

In the African American community, there is a stigma around talking to someone outside the family about our issues. It could be due to a lack of trust in others. It could be the financial costs associated with it. After all, therapy is not cheap! It could even be the hesitation to be vulnerable or to admit needing help, which is the antithesis of what it means to be "Black." Being Black in America has meant holding in the hurt and pain while being beaten and separated from our families during slavery. Being Black in America has meant enduring injustices committed upon us at the hands of lawmakers and people in power during the Civil Rights movement. We tend to believe these experiences of abuse and injustice are antiquated ones; however, they are still true to the Black experience in America, just with a different face and a new name. No wonder it has been hard to shake the SBW mentality that is passed down from generation to generation!

"I didn't want to end my life, but death seemed like the only cure for the excruciating pain of my broken heart."

Imagine going to the hospital for your open-heart surgery without receiving anesthetics prior to the operation. You would feel every incision and minuscule movement in your heart on an intensified level because you didn't have anything protecting you from the pain in advance. The separation from Deion felt this way and all I wanted was for the pain to end. Once we had worked through the initial shock of everything, I found myself talking about death a lot, especially after I found out Deion filed for divorce. I didn't want to end my life, but death seemed like the only cure for the excruciating pain of my broken heart.

My therapist was a Godsend because there was no holding back with her. From day one, we discussed spiritual and secular matters, especially as I learned practical ways of coping with all I was going through. I was honest regarding my truest feelings, fears, nightmares, and the unresolved childhood issues the separation ignited. It was no holds barred in our conversations. In fact, she was one of the people who encouraged me to be as authentic about my experience as I am in this book.

Another theme that surfaced during these authentic conversations with my therapist was my feeling of hopeless surrender. As a child, I loved watching the WWF and pretending to be a champion wrestler. I loved watching Brett "the Hitman" Hart, The Undertaker, Shawn Michaels, and other wresters in the ring defeating their opponents! I would try some of their moves during my imaginary matches in the ring of our living room. I'd jump off the couch as if I was jumping from the top rope before finishing off my imaginary opponent. Once I won the match, the imaginary ref would give me my championship belt, which was a bath towel, and I'd go to each corner of my living room ring riling up the fans and hearing the crowd roar in excitement!

But if you've ever watched wrestling, you know one of the most intense moments that draws the crowd in is when one wrestler pins the other by twisting his arm behind his back and forces him to tap out. Imagine the opponent who is bound, slowly lowering to the floor until they finally surrender the win. This was a constant mental image I had after receiving the advertisement from the divorce lawyers. Despite my mistakes and the issues Deion and I had, I felt forced into the divorce. I often told my therapist that I felt like I was in the fighting ring and Deion had my arm locked and I was forced to tap out of the marriage. Each week, we processed this further and she helped me reach the point where I felt empowered to make the choices I could with what I had remaining.

I know you may hesitate going to therapy and I realize not all therapists are created equal. Yet, I encourage anyone who is going through a rough season in life to seek out the help of a licensed therapist or mature counsel. Having a space where you can talk through your experience can help you make sounder decisions than thinking through things alone. If you are currently seeking help but your intuition says the counselor is not right for you, leave. You only inhibit your growth when you are unable to be transparent with God and at least one other person. In a storm, you may not know how to cope with your current issue, but you need to trust your level of comfort, and if the counselor doesn't make you feel safe and comfortable it won't work. Seek wise therapists or counselors to grow through what you are going through. Leave inadequate counseling relationships that do not nurture your development or ability to cope.

> Jesus said to him "If I will that he remain till I come, what is that to you? You follow Me."
> ~John 21:22

FOLLOW YOUR PURPOSE, NOT PEOPLE

Another way I learned to let go of my marriage was to focus on my purpose more than on what I had lost. This was not an easy task and the process of focusing on my purpose did not happen overnight. Throughout the separation and the divorce, I found myself consumed with concern about Deion's future. I wondered what he was thinking at any given moment. I questioned whether he was truly done with me. I even wondered if his heart was so cold that he could refuse to talk to me ever again.

DATING DADDY

One morning, I was reminded of John 21:22 when Jesus told Peter to not be concerned with another disciple's fate. Prior to this verse, Jesus told Peter how He would die and I assume Peter did not like hearing He would die in such a grim way. I assume Peter deflected like a child who didn't like being sent to timeout while his friends, who were with him, seemed to have a lighter sentence. Jesus responded that Peter, even after hearing unpleasant news, should not be concerned about anyone else, but to focus on following Him.

> "It doesn't seem fair that the people who wronged us seem to be more loved and have it easier than us in life."

In spiritual matters, how often do we look over the shoulders of Jesus to see what's going on with our fellow man? Do we notice Him trying to get our attention or are we too consumed by everyone else who may appear to have it better off than we do? How do we respond when God tells us our assignment as well as the challenges we will soon experience? What God reveals to us about our hard times may not seem fair, especially when we feel like we were wronged in life. It doesn't seem fair that the people who wronged us seem to be more loved and have it easier than us in life.

In my own situation, Jesus made it clear to me that my concern should be to follow Him and to not concern myself with Deion's fate. I needed to let go of the unforgiveness in my heart or holding on to ill thoughts about him. That I should surrender the thoughts and the worry about him facing the consequences of his actions. Why? Because our Heavenly Father loves both of us. There are no favorites with Him. Even though I felt like I was going through a lot more than Deion after he left, my primary focus was being redirected to Jesus and fulfilling His call in my life.

LEARNING TO LET GO

What was I to do while Deion seemed to be moving on to the next chapter of his life? I wish I could say I was able to bounce back immediately, but I would be lying. It appeared that Deion was doing well for himself while I went through the excruciating pain of my "shadow of death" experience and trying to recoup financially. There were many days I cried or was filled with so many tears that if a feather came across my skin, I'd be most likely to burst into tears uncontrollably. It took some time before I made it through a day without crying an ocean.

I came to realize Deion's departure may have been about issues bigger than me. That he was dealing with issues within and, though I may have offended him, he was fighting internal issues that were reflected back to him by our relationship. His issues may have had absolutely nothing to do with me. He had spoken of how tough his mother was on him, his perception of his father's love for his step-siblings, and his disgust of his ex whom he discovered was unfaithful to him. But at the end of the day, it was no longer my concern. My only concern was to follow Christ and to live out my new divine purpose.

My renewed love for God and revelation of Him as a Father was not a journey I would willingly choose to repeat, but it has transformed me in ways I would never imagine. I still make mistakes, but I am quick to acknowledge them instead of brushing them off as I did before. I no longer perform to try to earn the love of God or people. Instead, I am who I am and I realize God loves me despite my shortcomings. Instead of remaining in a place of low self-esteem and seeking the affirmation of others to build me up, now I welcome the confirmation from others about what God has already told me.

And my purpose? I don't know the "big purpose of my life," but I do know God is using my tests to form this testimony. Writing this book was both a reflection of my experiences and a process of healing that would never have been possible had I not surrendered the outcome of my marriage to God.

REALIZING DESTINY: SHARE YOUR STORY

It didn't take me long to realize there was nothing I could have done to keep my husband. Absolutely nothing. His departure was not a reflection of who I am. Though I am not perfect, I know that I am worthwhile. I know that who God has for me IS for me and someone who will fight for our union. It was hard to accept that my ex-husband was not a part of the destiny God had for my life. But once I redirected my focus from him to the things that would heal me, God resurrected old dreams and opened doors that would not have been available to me had I held on to what I lost.

Looking back on the story of the prodigal son, there's another angle we need to look at—the older brother's response to the father's joy upon his prodigal brother's return in Luke 15. If you're unfamiliar with the story, the older brother felt overlooked by his father because he had done all the right things. He'd been the perfect son: He was loyal to his father and was responsible. Yet he was not rewarded for his faithfulness. Like Peter, the older brother was overly concerned when it seemed he was getting the short end of the stick compared to his younger brother and all the lavish celebration he received upon his return. Similarly, I felt deep pain and neglect when Deion was offered the opportunity to resume the firefighting recruitment process the day after he left me. It was the same fire department that had denied him just months before our separation. Why did it seem he was being blessed after he abandoned our marriage?

What hurt me the most was that we were together when he actively pursued his dream and I supported him throughout every failed attempt. I pushed him to apply to every available recruitment opportunity even after he had given up on his dream. I felt I had invested so much into him, only to not be in the picture when his dream came true.

As I write this, I prayed to God about what I should leave you with. What shall I share with you, the reader, who may be going through a similar situation when the people who have mistreated you appear to be doing well while you're still trying to regain stability? It was then that He showed me Psalm 37:7. "Rest in the Lord, and wait patiently for Him; Do not fret because of him who prospers in his way…" It encourages us to rest in God and to not worry when it appears others' lives seem so amazing and better than ours. After reading that, I cried. It was as if God was saying to me, "Do not worry about Deion. It may appear that he is doing better than you, but rest in Me." That is no easy task, especially because I was still trying to bounce back financially and emotionally following the divorce.

> "I felt I had invested so much into him, only to not be in the picture when his dream came true."

Soon after this epiphany, God led me to Philippians 1:3. Paul and Timothy wrote to the church at Philippi and in that verse they said, "I thank God upon every remembrance of you." I continued reading until verse 11. Even though they were talking to the church, I felt like God was telling me to remember the good about Deion as another step in letting him go without bitterness. The words with which Paul and Timothy blessed the church at Philippi became my own benediction to Deion. Even in my hurt, it brought me a sense of peace to thank God for the good we had in our relationship.

Philippians 1 spoke to my heart and served as a reminder of why I needed to share my testimony. Looking back, I realize how much I have been healed. As I penned the remaining content for this book, I thought all the healing I needed was right here in these pages. It felt satisfying to know God healed me and there was nothing else to do. My work was done and I could begin turning a new leaf over in life without ever publishing this memoir.

But God was not through with me yet. He does not bring you through storms like the ones I've endured only to keep your story to yourself. It is important to share your testimony with others. That is where I found my purpose. Deion may have been able to live out his dream career, but I have found purpose through sharing my story of restoration from a time in my life that seemed insurmountable. I realized my destiny through experiences that appeared impossible to overcome. You too must help others by sharing your story as you are delivered from the trials you have overcome.

With that said, God has restored my self-image that was damaged in my relationship. He has healed me from hurts beyond my experience with Deion and He has already used my testimony to motivate others who have gone through or are going through similar circumstances. My heavenly Father, whom I now feel is near to me, has surrounded me with love overwhelming. Losing what I thought would last forever hurts. This experience has now become my own limp or thorn in my flesh. It is a constant reminder of that painful experience and it keeps me humble and not so quick to judge others like I would have before. This process of walking in my purpose has given me the hope to live out my destiny. I was destined to share this testimony with you. For that, I am grateful!

DAUGHTER OF THE MOST HIGH

Shavonne hitting a personal record for the clean & jerk at 64 kg (140.8 lbs) during the Indiana State Meet June 4, 2016

CHAPTER 21

BUILT TO LAST

HAVE YOU EVER HAD A friend you avoided telling something to because you feared they would respond a certain way? Well, Diana was that friend I didn't want to share the news about all that had gone on in my marriage. After all, she was in graduate school to become a marriage and family therapist and I didn't want her to use her techniques on me. When I finally opened up to her in March 2016, she proved to be a loving and supportive friend. After sharing my losses, my mother's health, and the divorce, she said something that helped me see my circumstances in another way. Diana said that God had been preparing me for the place I was in, in that very moment. I was taken aback. It would be later that I realized Diana's statement was not only true for the things she knew about my life, but it was also true for my private experience with God. He prepared me to stay strong in ways I almost overlooked before.

UNBROKEN

Looking back, I am reminded of a sermon my pastor preached, titled, "Unbroken" back in December before Deion and I went to court. Until this point, every sermon had helped me address the most recent issue I was dealing with in my life. I would come to church with a concern on my heart and my pastor would preach a relevant message that helped me answer that concern. It was as if God used my pastor as one of the people to guide me through my season of uncertainty.

In his sermon "Unbroken," Pastor Sullivan reminded us that part of being a follower of Christ includes suffering. His sermon covered 2 Corinthians 4:7-15 and Pastor explained Paul's difficulties, durability through his challenges, and his declaration for God's glory. Pastor reminded us that Paul's struggles strengthened the authenticity of his testimony and gave him credibility to speak of God's power. Instead of surrendering to the trials of life, Pastor reminded us that we were "built to last." Pastor Sullivan repeated that phrase several times throughout the sermon and they seemed to be a few of the only words I heard. Those words rung in my spirit every time he said them.

At the time of the sermon, my husband and I were a week and a half from our scheduled court mediation to divide our assets. I was a nervous wreck and I didn't think I could go on. When I heard the message "Unbroken," I felt as if it was God's way of telling me that my current experience would not break me. Whether we were to stay married or be divorced, I knew God would not allow me to bear more than I could. Yet there was a part of me that believed my marriage could not possibly be coming to an end.

Well actually, it did, and our "happily ever after" ended a couple of months before our second wedding anniversary. On top of that, my grief escalated with the loss of Uncle Mike, Uncle Moses, and my marriage within twenty-four hours and these events may impact me for as long as I live. God didn't save me from that pain. Being a Christian didn't protect me from the devastation and trauma I experienced. Making better choices didn't keep me from living through such hardships.

In my brokenness, I reacted emotionally in a social media post that reconnected me with my high school friend Kamille. The day after my social media outcry, Kamille invited me to a women's conference at her church. It took place days before

Mom'ela went to the hospital. The first session I attended was titled, "Still Standing," and this felt like God was adding to Pastor Sullivan's message before the trifecta of traumatic events interjected themselves. In the session, the leader shared practical ways to stand spiritually and she used principles of professional boxing to drive the message home. But the part of the conference that drove home the message I believed God was teaching me was the very last part. It was a mini-sermon where I adopted my life's quote for 2016 (which was used as the opening epigraph for this book by Sister Pamela Maddox). Guess what her sermon was titled? BUILT TO LAST!

> "We must shift our focus from the problem to the God who loves us and can bring us through any situation."

I was so captivated by the Sister Maddox's message that I didn't write as many notes as I usually do. But what I do remember is that it takes tenacity to keep pressing when life is trying to take you under. We must shift our focus from the problem to the God who loves us and can bring us through any situation. During the conference, I believe God led me to a scripture that would remind me this was not the end for me.

> *I would have lost heart, unless I had believed that I would see the goodness of the Lord in the land of the living. Wait on the Lord; Be of good courage, And He shall strengthen your heart; Wait, I say, on the Lord!*
> ~Psalm 27:13-14

It is easier to lose hope when it seems you will never have the victory, but if we remember God's unconditional love we can hold on to hope. Our victory is assured! We can believe He will bring us through EVERYTHING. Absolutely everything! He will strengthen us through the storms of life. But the strength is not limited to what He develops within us. The transformation God propels within us can also be evident in our physical strength.

STRENGTH PERSONIFIED

After four months of focused training, I prepared for my first USA Weightlifting competition at the Indiana State Meet. The day before the competition was an emotional day. I took the day off work to relax and prepare my gym bag with snacks and other items needed for the competition. That morning, I had an appointment with my therapist. During the session, I shared some things that brought tears to my eyes. I recounted a few of the life events leading up to the competition, including the divorce and shadow of death experience of January 2016. My therapist mentioned how my tears seemed different now—that they were not as heavy as they once were. I tried to stop them but they flowed like a light mist. My therapist ended the session suggesting they were probably the release I needed before the competition.

For anyone who's been to therapy regularly, you know that some days you can walk out and return to life as normal. It's as if you pressed pause on life, talked about your emotional concerns, and pressed play as you leave the session. Other times, there is this thing my therapist refers to as the "therapy hangover." It's when you've talked about your feelings and issues during the session, but that openness and emotional vulnerability remain open and follow you home. I've felt that many times before, especially as I processed the separation. I could not shake the emotional heaviness from our sessions until a day or two later.

Following the pre-competition therapy session, I returned home and experienced what I would call a deep emotional sensation. It appeared to be the onset of a therapy hangover.

It started after I put down my bags in the condo and looked down at my right wrist where I wore two rubber bracelets. On Mother's Day, my mother had given me a pink bracelet representing her survival from breast cancer. The other bracelet she gave me was green from her overcoming Hodgkin's Lymphoma just this year. One look down at my wrist and I began to cry in praise. Those little bracelets represented survival. Not only had Mom'ela survived, but her Baby Girl survived. I had a private worship service right there in the living room in which I thanked God for ALL He brought me THROUGH and by the end, I dedicated my competition to my mother.

The next morning, on June 4, 2016, I woke up before 6 a.m. to the news that "the greatest of all time" heavyweight boxing champion Muhammed Ali had passed away the night before. I paused. I could have taken a deeper meaning behind the timing of his passing as it was the day before my first competition. Nevertheless, this was a legend who I've often quoted to press through my physical training as well as at this point in my life. My favorite quote of Ali's talks about how anything is possible and minimizes those things we fear. He ends the quote by saying,

Impossible is nothing.

This quote was the screensaver on my phone for months, including the morning I learned of his passing. His legacy is one of greatness. He believed in himself and stuck true to his morals without compromise. He did not let down in the ring and I kept that in mind as I headed to the site of my first Olympic Lifting competition.

I was a nervous wreck at check-in, but I made weight! I weighed 73 kg, which was in my weight class of 68-75 kg. At least two weeks before, I was nervous I would not weigh in my classification and began to eat more of a paleo-like diet until the competition. The fear of not making weight was enough to keep me focused on nutrition, but this was not the only source of my anxiety. I was also nervous because I was wearing a singlet in front of people. Total complete strangers. If you're not familiar with the official weightlifting gear, this is a sleeveless, tight-fitting body suit that reveals almost as much as a one-piece swimsuit. And it was not your regular solid-colored singlet. It had to mean something to me so I ordered a singlet that represented me best during this season in life. The design was called "love voodoo doll" and it had the appearance of patches stitched together with a heart patched on at the top. Needless to say, it was pro-vo-ca-tive! Coach Red would later say it reminded him of something from the film *The Nightmare Before Christmas*.

After weigh-in, another athlete from my box and I warmed up together. She had a competition or two under her belt and she gave me tips for the flow of the day. After being stuck in traffic, Coach Red arrived within minutes of the starting time and strategized the plans for our lifts. After the athletes did introductions, I put in my earphones and warmed up with Beyoncé's song "Formation" on repeat between the warm-up reps.

The first lift was the "snatch," which requires the athlete to lift the barbell from the ground to overhead in one continuous motion with a wide grip on the bar. I beat my personal record by hitting 50 kilograms just days before, but I thought it unlikely I would hit that under the pressure of the lights. Well, my approach to the platform on the first two attempts, though successful, was not as calculated as the other athletes. Immediately, I studied how my competitors approached the bar and found my own rhythm by my third successful attempt. During the break between the first and second half, my friends Shawnee, Kori, and

DATING DADDY

Riley said I looked as if I could have lifted more weight. They always teased that I dropped the bar like it was nothing—as if I said, "Hey, I lifted it (drops bar) now it's time to do brunch" or something else so nonchalantly.

After the break, the next lift was the clean and jerk. It is a two-part movement. The first, the clean, is when the barbell is lifted from the ground, caught on top of the shoulders, and ends with the weightlifter standing straight up and the barbell on the clavicle. The second part, the jerk, is when the weight is propelled upwards, and is caught with arms straight overhead. Back at my home box, I failed to hit 61 kg after multiple attempts. Today, I was going to attempt 64 kg, which is 140.8 pounds. I didn't know how it was going to happen, but I was going to try. My first attempt on the platform was at 58 kg. All I remember was that I approached the bar, looked for the judge's signal of approval to lift, gripped the bar, breathed, and POW! With each lift, I mentally blacked out, remembering nothing during the execution. I did this during the snatch and now I was doing it during the clean and jerk. It wasn't until I saw the judge's gesture signaling a completed lift that I regained awareness of where I was.

My next attempt was 61 kg. With my newly established approach, I walked to the loaded bar and planted my feet under the bar where I practiced so many times before. After receiving approval from the judge, I bent my knees and began the lift. I braced my core before lifting the bar when I noticed a toddler walking across the front row in my peripheral view. Without standing up, I refocused, reset my breath and lifted the bar.

A success! I could not hit that weight before, but I did it in this meet. Somewhere between my first and third attempt, the loaders (those whose job it is to add weights to the bar) put on blue plates. Each blue was 20 kg and the sight of them scared me.

I had not graduated to blue. The blue plates are for the elite athletes at my box. Not me.

What the what?

How could I lift the Big Blues?

I was a nervous wreck!

Ok. Calm down, Shavonne.

Remember the basics.

> "Remember the basics."

I took a deep breath and prepared for my final lift. When the announcer introduced me and said it was my final attempt, everyone in that room cheered me on. From my four friends who were in attendance and people from my gym to the other athletes and their families who were there to support them. They all started cheering for me. I heard, "Go Shavonne!" as I approached the platform.

If they only knew.

I grinned. Took a breath. Approached the bar and awaited the judge's approval to make my final lift. I exhaled and initiated the lift. At the bottom of the "clean," the weight was too heavy. I struggled as I pressed down on my legs and made it to standing position.

Now it was time to complete the second part of the movement: the "jerk"—to get 64 kilograms, 140.8 American pounds, over my head. More than 140 pounds was about to be over my head if I could just complete this final lift. I took several deep breaths to recover with the bar and weights racked on my shoulders.

Remember the basics.

I took my final breath. Braced. Punched the bar in the air like my coaches said in training. Returned my feet to parallel position with the bar over my head. The judge gave his final approval and I dropped that bar immediately.

There was thunderous clapping. I walked toward my proud coach with the biggest grin on my face. I had not smiled the entire competition. I did it! I lifted something I have never lifted before. I achieved what I never thought I could. Then I thought about all I had lived through the last ten months. I survived things that could have taken me out. This competition was my revenant experience! Shavonne was coming back!

Coach Red gave me a high-five and said, "We have to train you harder!"

And I walked away exhausted, but still smiling.

BEAUTY FOR ASHES

When I started training for my first weightlifting competition, no one could have told me I would have been able to lift that amount of weight. I didn't make every attempt in training, but with patience and by trusting my coaches' process, I was ready to conquer what I had not been able to do before. Outside of the box, I had to experience everything I did to make me stronger and to live out God's purpose for my life. Because He kept me when I gave up on myself, I can share the good news of His unconditional love more effectively than I ever could when I was always "happy." The pain validated my testimony and gave it sincerity and authenticity.

I was ashamed of what I had gone through. There were times where the depression, financial hardship, and a conglomerate of other things kept me from showing my face. I don't want to minimize the realities of my situation or mental illness but I couldn't hide in shame forever. You, too, will reach a point in your healing where it is no longer okay to hide. One of my favorite quotes by Joyce Meyer is "Do it afraid." The shame will be there. The fear will be there. But sometimes you need to take the leap and do whatever frightens you with shaky legs and abnormal twitching. Only then can you step into the new territory God has for you.

One of my first acts of walking toward my fear was the wedding-inspired photoshoot.

In retrospect, the photograph used for the cover of this book has taken on a new meaning. In the moment when those images were captured, I was lost and didn't know if my own marriage would survive in the midst of the separation. I believed this was a normal part of holy matrimony and that our marriage would recover from this storm. It's not uncommon for marriages to go through seasons like this, right? I believed we would look back on this time and say, Look what we overcame. But with each pose and angle during the shoot, I struggled through the uncertainty of my marriage, my next moves, and my identity.

Who was I to wear my wedding dress when my marriage had fallen apart?

Yet, God has a way of exchanging the ashes of our losses for beauty and renewal (Isaiah 61:3). He can take what seems to be a damaging situation in life to propel us to greatness. If I had my druthers, I would not have gone through all I faced to learn these lessons. However, the healing process taught me a father's unconditional love goes beyond himself to care for his children. I did not understand this. I could not comprehend this as a daughter who grew up without her father for most of her life. What I do know is that when I was at the end of hope and had no will of my own to persist, God's love as a Father became clear to me. My Heavenly Father was intimate with me in a way I could never be in a relationship, including the one I thought was going to last until death do us part. Like a good father, He allowed me to come back into His arms to cry, to heal, and provided the foundation to start again.

After the struggles I had experienced and especially in

DATING DADDY

January 2016, I wondered what would be the consolation for all of this? What is the reward for pressing on? There's not a major award for surviving life. No standing ovation for overcoming life's obstacles.

Months later, I came to realize what the prize was. It wasn't something I would have imagined it to be. The gift was something so clear but easy for me to overlook. It was easy to overlook when I believed I was a victim of my daddy issues and bad romance. But now that I have overcome, I realize it is the greatest gift of all: I know what God's unconditional love feels like and there is nothing that can change that. More than anything, I realized the greatest gift having survived what I thought was insurmountable:

> *"There's not a major award for surviving life. No standing ovation for overcoming life's obstacles."*

I.
AM.
STILL.
HERE!

ADDENDUM: Being a Loving Bystander

Before I experienced the devastation of my marital issues, I associated with a lot of people. But when I was experiencing the events of my "shadow of death" season, my inner circle was reduced to three friends: Tamara "Chrisette" Jordan, Manon "Riley" Bullock, and Jasmine "Kori" Kelly.

These ladies were in my corner when I was most vulnerable. They witnessed many of my tears, my battle with depression, and the effort it took for me to do the simplest of tasks. Tamara, Manon, and Jasmine were bystanders to one of the darkest seasons of my life. A bystander is someone who witnesses something but is not involved in the process. None of these women have been married before, but their support was more than enough for me. Meanwhile, I kept people away who hurt me with unloving words and statements that were offensive to me.

Maybe you are a bystander to the journey of someone you love and you don't know how to be there for them. I've compiled a short, and not exhaustive, list of things to do and to avoid when trying to support a friend who is grieving the loss of a marriage, person, or opportunity:

- Do listen intently. Hear what your friend has to say without interruption.
- Don't generalize what is being said. Your attempt to empathize may be diminishing to your friend.
- Do encourage them to take care of themselves with adequate rest, eating, and regular exercise.
- Don't villainize the ex or the lost opportunity. Obviously, your friend loved them at one point.
- Do encourage them to talk, but…

- Don't force the conversation. Sometimes awkward silence is more effective than talking.
- Do hug your friend (only if they are a hugger). Physical touch isn't everyone's love language.
- Don't ask them about the status of their ex or if they have spoken with them. Period.
- Don't take on your friend's grief or pain. Do take care of yourself and know your limitations.
- Do pray for your friend and send them words of encouragement regularly.

ACKNOWLEDGEMENTS

First and foremost, I would like to thank God. There were chapters and content in this book that You inspired even before my healing came in those areas. You loved me so much You surrounded me with loving experiences, loving people, and a peace that surpasses...well, you know the rest. Every good thing about my healing and this work, I owe it all to You.

To my mother, thank you for your sacrifices and for teaching me the art of bouncing back. I have gained the courage to start again and again and again if necessary. To my sister, I love you and my beautiful niece. You both have given me purpose since the day you were born. To my GMa, you know you are my heart! I appreciate you for molding me and teaching me the lessons as a child that I practice today. I love you!

I'd like to pay homage to the men who have served as fathers and wise counsel to me:

    Paul William Barrett
    Dennis Bland, Esq.
    Cornelius Bullock
    William Caise
    Uncle Keith Clemons
    Mark Edwards
    Charles Jackson - GPa
    Robert Jackson
    Thomas Dexter "T.D." Jakes
    Jeffrey A. Johnson, Sr.
    Roger Jordan, Sr.
    Uncle Murray Stewart
    Pastor Kenneth E. Sullivan, Jr.
    Uncle Phil "P Diddy" Warner

ACKNOWLEDGEMENTS

Thank you, Soror Lynnette Barrett, Maurice Williams Jr., Richard Okello, Rachel Ogorek, Tarah Sanders, and Rachel Becker for reading through the rough drafts. Thank you, Sophia Muthuraj and Janet Schwind for your editorial services. This project was near and dear to me and you were sensitive to that while challenging me to improve my ability to convey the meaning behind this healing work. Thank you, Sylvia "Ess" Rivers, for capturing my vision with your cover design. Thank you Suzanne Parada for your beautiful work with the interior design.

My deepest gratitude to Laurie Budlong-Morse. Thank you for helping me process life after the separation and for being available beyond our sessions. You have helped my healing process, extinguished fires (wow!), and allowed me to be more gracious to myself.

To my family, you have showed up for me in ways you cannot understand! Thanks for being a shoulder to cry on and to remind me of the girl you helped to mold. Thanks, Aunt Lisa Davis, for sharing your journey with me and for showing me I was not alone. Thank you to my "big sister" cousin, Monique Davis, for telling me there would be purpose behind my pain. Thank you, Aunt Val Stewart, for always going above and beyond for me.

To my AMAZING colleagues, Angie Murphy and Mike Kane. Thank you for opening your hearts and home to me. Thank you, James "Irish Jimmy" Condron for the laughs as well. To Vanessa Pacheco, our carpool duet sessions have freed my spirit. Thank you for bearing with me during my emotional days and for giving me the space to ride out my emotions. To Ryan "the Hype Man" Davis, thank you for your sense of humor during those rides.

My deepest gratitude to all the angels on earth who lifted me when I did not have the energy to lift my wings: Erin Adafin, Brandy Bennett, Kelisha Chandler, Antonia Dangerfield,

Brittany Davis, DeShara Doub, Dyla Harris, Jasmine Kelly, Anyah Land, Damar McMurray, Stacey Miller-Jones, Jasmin Pettigrew, Brandi Rice, Shalisa Richards, Courtney Rousseau, Teresha Twyman, and a few others. I was never alone because one or more of you called (stalked) me throughout my valley experience. God sent each of you at the right moment to keep me pushing. If YOU only knew…you all saved a life! All I can say is thank you!

Thank you to my "other mothers" who helped to raise me including Mrs. Felecia Jordan, Mrs. Evelyn Bullock, and a few others.

A special thank you to the team who was a part of the Haute Couture Events photoshoot on the cover. Thank you, Shanbri' Cade, Lacoiya Reed, Soror Kori Morgan, Sabrena Suggs, and Quintin Ross. You all made me feel most beautiful in the midst of a storm and you did not even know it!

Thank you to Coach Jeff Edwards and the coaching staff of Broad Ripple Fit Club. You "saw" me during a time I felt most invisible.

Thank you, Soror Jessica Collins, Danita Dolly, Courtney and Kendall Hamilton, LaToya Johnson, Anyah Land, Anna Ruel, Nolan "NoVonne" Ryan, Jason Richardson, and all who made financial contributions to bring this book forward. I appreciate your belief in me and a dream.

Thank you, Dad, Cliff, Leo, and Deion for the lessons.

Most of all, I am grateful to you, the reader, for taking the time to read this testimony. My hope is that you learn from both my shortcomings and the lessons learned along the way. Feel free to share this with others as you are led. Thank you!

R.I.P. Uncle Moses Tolbert

NOTES

PREFACE

Ed Gordon, "Daddy's Still Got You," *Essence*, July 2016, p. 118.

CHAPTER 2: FATHER(S) FOR THE FATHERLESS

Best, Sarah. *"Healing the Father Daughter Relationship."* Health and Happiness, Holistically. Accessed May 22, 2016 http://www.sarahbesthealth.com/healing-father-daughter-relationship/

Bowlby, John. "Attachment and Loss: Retrospect and Prospect." American Journal of Orthopsychiatry 52, no. 4 (October 1982): 664-678. American Psychological Association. Reprinted with permission. APA is not responsible for the accuracy of this translation.

Coley, R. L. (2003). "Daughter-Father Relationships and Adolescent Psychosocial Functioning in Low-Income African American Families." Journal of Marriage and Family, 65: 867–875.

Freud, Sigmund. https://www.brainyquote.com/quotes/quotes/s/sigmundfre138674.html (accessed May 15, 2016)

Secunda, Victoria, Women and their Fathers: The Sexual and Roman*tic Impact of the First Man of Your Life* (New York: Delta, 1993), p.199.

CHAPTER 3: MAKING MEANING OF GOD, THE PROVIDER

Eunice Matthews-Armstead "Daughters' Constructions of Connectedness to Their Nonresident Father." *The Myth of the Missing Black Father,* ed. Roberta L. Coles and Charles Green. (New York: Columbia University Press, 2010), 261-278.

CHAPTER 5: SILVER LINING

Booth, Alan, Mindy E Scott, and Valarie King. "Father Residence and Adolescent Problem Behavior: Are Youth Always Better Off in Two-Parent Families?" Journal of Family Issues 31, no. 5 (2010): 585-605

Houston-Little, Janice Marie. African-American Men and Their Daughters: Living out the Father-daughter Drama. Bloomington, IN: AuthorHouse, 2008.

Julion, Wrenetha, Deborah Gross, Gina Barclay- McLaughlin, and Louis Fogg. "It's Not Just about MOMMAS": African- American Non- resident Fathers' Views of Paternal Involvement." Research in Nursing & Health 30, no. 6 (2007): 595-610.

Good Reads "Elvis Presley Quotes" Accessed July 7, 2016 http://www.goodreads.com/quotes/276452-when-things-go-wrong-don-t-go-with-them.

Secunda, Victoria. Women and Their Fathers: The Sexual and Romantic Impact of the First *Man in Your Life*. (New York: Delta, 1993), p. 9.

CHAPTER 8: CAN YOU SEE (THE REAL) ME?

Donovan, Roxanne A., and Lindsey M. West. "Stress and Mental Health: Moderating Role of the Strong Black Woman Stereotype." Journal of Black Psychology 41, no. 4 (2015): 384-96.

Eunice Matthews-Armstead "Daughters' Constructions of Connectedness to Their Nonresident Father." The Myth of the Missing Black Father, ed. Roberta L. Coles and Charles Green. (New York: Columbia University Press, 2010), 261-278.

Nielsen, Linda. "College Daughters' Relationships with Their

Fathers: A 15-year study." College Student Journal, 2007, vol 41, accessed May 20, 2016, http://users.wfu.edu/nielsen/15%20yr%20article.pdf

Punyanunt-Carter, Narissra Maria. "Using Attachment Theory to Study Communication Motives in Father–Daughter Relationships." Communication Research Reports 24, no. 4 (2007): 311-18.

Shorter-Gooden, Kumea and N. Chanell Washington. "Young, Black, and Female: The Challenge of Weaving an Identity." *Journal of Adolescence* 19, no. 5 (1996): 465-75.

CHAPTER 11: NATURE OF THE CHASE

Antfolk, Salo, Alanko, Bergen, Corander, Sandnabba, and Santtila. "Women's and Men's Sexual Preferences and Activities with Respect to the Partner's Age: Evidence for Female Choice." *Evolution and Human Behavior* 36, no. 1 (2015): 73-79.

Casterline, John B., Lindy Williams, and Peter McDonald. "The Age Difference Between Spouses: Variations among Developing Countries." *Population Studies* 40, no. 3 (1986): 353-74.

Dunn, Michael J., Brinton, Stacey, and Clark, Lara. "Universal Sex Differences in Online Advertisers Age Preferences: Comparing Data from 14 Cultures and 2 Religious Groups." Evolution and Human Behavior 31, no. 6 (2010): 383.

Luke N. "Confronting the 'Sugar Daddy' Stereotype: Age and Economic Asymmetries and Risky Sexual Behavior in Urban Kenya." International Family Planning Perspectives, 2005, 31(1):6-14, https://www.guttmacher.org/about/journals/ipsrh/2005/03/confronting-sugar-daddy-stereotype-age-and-economic-asymmetries-and.

Mehta, Vinita Ph.D. "When It Comes to Dating, Do Age

Differences Matter?" Psychology Today. Accessed July 10, 2016. https://www.psychologytoday.com/blog/head-games/201308/when-it-comes-dating-do-age-differences-matter

Ross, Jasmine N., and Nicole M. Coleman. "Gold Digger or Video Girl: The Salience of an Emerging Hip-hop Sexual Script." Culture, Health & Sexuality 13, no. 2 (2011): 157-71.

Secunda, Victoria. Women and Their Fathers: The Sexual and Romantic Impact of *the First Man of Your Life* (New York: Delta, 1993), p.213.

CHAPTER 15: LOVING ON EGGSHELLS

Bowlby, John. "Attachment and loss: Retrospect and prospect." American Journal of Orthopsychiatry 52, no. 4 (October 1982): 664-678. American Psychological Association. Reprinted with permission. APA is not responsible for the accuracy of this translation.

Hooper, Lisa M. "The Application of Attachment Theory and Family Systems Theory to the Phenomena of Parentification." Family Journal 15, no. 3 (2007): 217-24.

Johnson, R. Skip (13 July 2014). "Codependency and Codependent Relationships." BPDFamily.com. http://bpdfamily.com/content/codependency-codependent-relationships Retrieved 16 August 2016.

Madden, Amber R, and Anne Shaffer. "The Relation Between Parentification and Dating Communication." The Family Journal 24, no. 3 (2016): 313-18.

McFadden, Joyce. "3 Things Little Girls Need from Their Fathers." Huffington Post. Published June 18, 2013. Updated August 18, 2013. Accessed May 22, 2016 http://www.huffingtonpost.com/joyce-mcfadden/things-little-girls-need-from-their-fathers_b_3348956.html.

Stephens, Dionne, and A. Few. "The Effects of Images of African American Women in Hip Hop on Early Adolescents' Attitudes toward Physical Attractiveness and Interpersonal Relationships." *Sex Roles* 56, no. 3 (2007): 251-64.

Wells, Marolyn, Cheryl Glickauf-Hughes, and Rebecca Jones. "Codependency: A Grass Roots Construct's Relationship to Shame-proneness, Low Self-esteem, and Childhood Parentification." *The American Journal of Family Therapy* 27, no. 1 (1999): 63-71.

CHAPTER 16: UNRAVELING A FORTUITOUS MARRIAGE

Bowlby, John. "Attachment and loss: Retrospect and prospect." *American Journal of Orthopsychiatry* 52, no. 4 (October 1982): 664-678. American Psychological Association. Reprinted with permission. APA is not responsible for the accuracy of this translation.

Thomas, Gary. https://www.facebook.com/AuthorGaryThomas/posts/612224655525068 Retrieved 15 October 15, 2016.

CHAPTER 18: A FATHER'S JOY: DAUGHTER'S RESTORATION

Aaron A. Smith. "Standing in the 'GAP'." *The Myth of the Missing Black Father*, ed. Roberta L. Coles and Charles Green. (New York: Columbia University Press, 2010), 170-191.

ABOUT THE AUTHOR

Shavonne Holton is founder and CEO of VK Press, a publishing company with the aim of connecting independent authors with freelance artists to create globally published content. Although *Dating Daddy* is her first published work, she has been writing since the age of nine when she began songwriting. She received her BA in Theatre from Purdue University and her MS Ed. in Higher Education and Student Affairs from Indiana University (but she is a Boilermaker at heart). She has a reputation for finding the beauty in all things and this is the muse for the creation of her blog *All Things Inspiration*. Holton lives in the Midwest and thoroughly enjoys weightlifting, live performances, traveling, movies (including the bonus footage behind the production process) and trying new restaurants.

www.ingramcontent.com/pod-product-compliance
Lightning Source LLC
Chambersburg PA
CBHW030433010526
44118CB00011B/619